ALPHABET BOOKS

The K–12 Educators' Power Tool

Bonnie Mackey and Hedy Schiller Watson

LIBRARIES
UNLIMITED™

An Imprint of ABC-CLIO, LLC

Santa Barbara, California • Denver, Colorado

Library of Congress Cataloging-in-Publication Data

Names: Mackey, Bonnie, author. | Watson, Hedy Schiller, author.
Title: Alphabet books : the K-12 educators' power tool / Bonnie Mackey and Hedy Schiller Watson.
Description: Santa Barbara, California : Libraries Unlimited, [2017] |
    Includes bibliographical references and index.
Identifiers: LCCN 2016022024 (print) | LCCN 2016042361 (ebook) | ISBN
    9781440841620 (paperback) | ISBN 9781440841637 (ebook)
Subjects: LCSH: Alphabet books—Bibliography. | Alphabet books.
Classification: LCC Z1033.H8 M33 2017 (print) | LCC Z1033.H8 (ebook) | DDC
    411—dc23
LC record available at https://lccn.loc.gov/2016022024

ISBN: 978-1-4408-4162-0
EISBN: 978-1-4408-4163-7

21 20 19 18 17   1 2 3 4 5

This book is also available as an eBook.

Libraries Unlimited
An Imprint of ABC-CLIO, LLC

ABC-CLIO, LLC
130 Cremona Drive, P.O. Box 1911
Santa Barbara, California 93116-1911
www.abc-clio.com

This book is printed on acid-free paper ∞
Manufactured in the United States of America

To my five granddaughters:

Lorelei **A**nnabel **A**shley

Sophia **K**atherine

Who are the important letters in Nana's alphabet
—Bonnie Mackey

To Jim and our wonderful children Julia and Alistair, with love.
Aren't we lucky!
—Hedy Schiller Watson

Contents

Acknowledgments

It was during one of Dr. Bonnie Mackey's classes at the University of Houston Clear Lake that Rose Toman, a graduate student, created a unique and clever alphabet book about the national spelling bee. That class project inspired Dr. Mackey to pursue research on alphabet books. Realizing the wealth of instructional opportunities that alphabet books could present to librarians and classroom teachers, she recognized the need for an inclusive resource about alphabet books.

We also acknowledge and appreciate the contributions of Dr. Wade C. Mackey as a reader of several drafts and as a constant source of suggestions that improved our thinking and ultimately our writing. Thank you, PawPaw! We also acknowledge Teia Baker for her assistance and support.

The coauthors are grateful for the assistance of the staff at the Rare Book and Special Collection of the Library of Congress. In particular, we thank Cheryl Adams, reference specialist, and Dr. Sybille Jagusch, chief of the Children's Literature Center.

Last, but certainly not least, we would like to thank all of the thousands of moms, dads, and caregivers who read alphabet books each day (and night) to their children. The foundation for literacy learning is being developed by their constant vigilance over their children's educational success.

Introduction

With an extensive listing of over 300 alphabet books and their summaries, *Alphabet Books: The K–12 Educators' Power Tool* provides librarians and classroom educators with an inclusive and invaluable resource for their curricular and instructional uses. Within the pages of this book, alphabet books are arranged according to topics for quick and easy reference. In addition, each listed book has a brief summary of its content, including a discussion of its illustrations, identification of its content area, and its instructional value for designated grade levels.

The authors delineated three major categories of text structure found within alphabet books. These three text structures are

1. Single letter
2. Hidden letters
3. Conceptual text

Within each category, the authors chose a representative book and developed an instructional activity for each of three grade levels (prekindergarten through second, third through sixth, and seventh through twelfth) to accompany the selected book. Clear, concise instructions for implementing each of the nine instructional activities, along with photographs of the nine completed products, are presented.

With the burgeoning population of international students and multicultural classrooms, interest in ESL (English as a Second Language) has increased. Chapter 6 is devoted to alphabet books for Spanish speakers, with specific instructional activities and Web sites presented to support ELLs (English Language Learners).

Librarians, teachers, parents, and caregivers will find *Alphabet Books: The K–12 Educators' Power Tool* valuable for the following reasons:

- A brief history of the English alphabet, with accompanying Web sites
- Information about the history of alphabet books, with accompanying Web sites

- Three categories of text structure within alphabet books
- Nine instructional activities with photographs for implementing alphabet books
- Summaries of over 300 alphabet books, arranged by topic
- Three student-centered instructional activities with photographs for scaffolding English Language Learners

Chapter 1

History of the English Alphabet

If you leave alphabet soup on the stove and go out, it could spell disaster.
Michael Rosen in *Alphabetical: How Every Letter Tells a Story*

What Is an Alphabet?

What is an alphabet? "A list, in a particular order, of all the letters used in a language is called an alphabet" (Robb, p. 7). For thousands of years, people used pictures to describe events and ideas. As it became increasingly difficult to relay abstract terms like "beautiful" or "truly" using drawings, ancient peoples cleverly turned pictures into symbols. Logographic writing systems are based on the principle of each written symbol representing a concept, as opposed to phonographic or alphabetic systems, in which each written symbol represents a sound of the language. Alphabetic writing systems need fewer symbols than ones based on logograms. Eventually, these written symbols represented the sounds of the language. These "sound pictures" are called letters. "Each language has thousands and thousands of words, but only a limited number of sounds. So each language needs relatively few letters" (Robb, p. 7).

Alphabet Beginnings in 2000 BC

Scholars who have studied the history of languages confirm that our English alphabet can be traced back about 4,000 years (around 2000 BC) (Man; Sacks, *Language Visable*). The alphabet we use today had its origins in the ancient Middle East and its surroundings. Beginning as picture symbols (hieroglyphs) in Egypt in 2000 BC, these letters were borrowed by the people of the Sinai Peninsula and developed into an alphabet of about 18 letters. This alphabet was adapted by the Phoenicians, who, through their extensive trading with other cultures, spread it to various trading partners, including the Greeks. The Greeks developed their own shapes for the Phoenician alphabet and even added some of their own letters. By 800 BC, the Greek alphabet was the one used in government and business throughout the Mediterranean area. By around 200 BC, the Romans had overpowered the Greeks as the dominant culture in the Mediterranean world. They adapted the Greek alphabet to align with their growing empire. This 23-letter Latin alphabet (without J, U, or W) traveled with the Roman Empire as it expanded into Europe, including Britain (Man; Robb).

Alphabet Additions

"Adapting the Latin alphabet to English meant the addition of extra letters. The result was a phonetic system in which every letter was sounded" (Crystal, p. 20). Both U and V appeared as consonants and as vowels. V was often found at the beginning of words, and U was found as a vowel in the middle of words. When the distinction became standard in the late 1600s, the V was reserved as a consonant (primarily), and U was used as a vowel (Crystal).

The letter W was introduced in the 11th century by Norman scribes to represent the sound /w/. Note that the grapheme is composed of two V's while its name sounds like "double U," reflecting the interchangeability of V and U in Middle English (Crystal).

The youngest of the letters to join the current English alphabet is the letter J. Scholars of linguistics have differing views regarding the creation of the letter J, but most believe that the written letter J entered the English alphabet about 400–500 years ago (Crystal; Man; Sacks, *The Alphabet*) as monks transcribed the letter I with an elongated tail. Gradually, J began to replace I when that letter represented a consonant. The distinction between lowercase J and lowercase I became standard in the 1600s, but the uppercase distinction was not accepted as standard until the 1800s (Crystal; Sacks, *Letter Perfect*)!

The English Alphabet Today

All languages in existence today contain from 20 to 44 phonemes. A phoneme is the smallest unit of speech sound within any specific language (Finegan). In the 26-letter English language, there are 44 phonemes and 26 graphemes (Crystal; Reutzel and Cooter). Consider each of the 26 letters (written symbols or graphemes) as having at least one sound, and then add unique, new sounds of digraphs like /ph/ and diphthongs like /ou/.

The Future of the English Alphabet

"It's never wise to predict the future, when it comes to language" (Crystal, p. 270). Will the 26-letter English alphabet remain intact as rapidly growing technologies such as the Internet, Twitter, and texting become mainstays of communication? If the English alphabet adds or deletes a letter, so goes the future of alphabet books.

"A B C D, E F G . . . H I J K, L M N O P . . . Q R S, T U V . . . W, X, Y and Z. Now I know my ABCs, won't you come and sing with me?" Who created this famous alphabet song? The composer is unknown, but Charles Bradee, a music publisher, first copyrighted the song in 1835. The alphabet song contains refrains from *Twelve Variations on "Ah vous dirai-je, Maman,"* one of Mozart's compositions, and shares the tune of "Twinkle, Twinkle, Little Star" and "Baa, Baa, Black Sheep."

Books for Students

Czekaj, Jef. *A Call for a New Alphabet.* New York: Charlesbridge, 2011. Print.

Dubosarsky, Ursula. *The Word Snoop.* New York: Dial, 2009. Print.

Fisher, Leonard Everett. *Alphabet Art: Thirteen ABCs from Around the World.* New York: Four Winds, 1978. Print.

Isabella, Jude. *Chitchat: Celebrating the World's Languages.* Tonawanda, NY: Kids Can Press, 2013. Print.

Robb, Don. *Ox, House, Stick: The History of Our Alphabet* (A. Smith, Illus.). Watertown, MA: Charlesbridge, 2007. Print.

Rossi, R. *The Revolution of the Alphabet (Reading and Writing).* New York: Marshall Cavendish, 2009. Print.

Samoyault, Tiphaine. *Alphabetical Order: How the Alphabet Began.* New York: Viking, 1998. Print.

Librarians' Link

Within most elementary school libraries, the letters of our English alphabet are posted on a wall or bulletin board. The actual word "alphabet" derives from *alpha* and *beta*, the first two letters of the Greek alphabet. Although the Romans originally had named their list of letters *literae* (letters) or *elementa* (elements), they began using the word *alphabetum* around the third century BC when they became the important power in the Mediterranean world (Robb).

Listed below are useful and interesting Web sites about the development of several alphabets for librarians to share with teachers and students.

Notable Web Sites

http://www.ancientscripts.com/alphabet.html

This informative Web page is targeted at teachers and students of grades 7 through 12. Packed with historical information about the development of several alphabets, this Web page possesses a distinct appeal to those educators who want to know more about our

(continued)

(*continued*)

Roman alphabet, its origin, and its transformation. A heavy use of linguistic terms adds to the Web page's worth for the inquisitive teacher and student.

http://www.history.com/news/ask-history/who-created-the-first-alphabet

This three-minute video describes the evolution of our English alphabet. This video can serve as an excellent introduction to the study of the alphabet for middle-grade students.

http://www.historian.net/hxwrite.htm

This Web page not only portrays the history of our alphabet but also includes visual images of authentic ancient written language, such as ancient cylinder seals and the consonants of the Egyptian alphabet. Teachers and students of grades 5 through 12 will enjoy the clarity and artwork of this Web page.

http://www.edinformatics.com/inventions_inventors/alphabet.htm

The value of this Web page lies in its clear, concise explanations of somewhat complex and controversial linguistic terms and concepts. Educators and students in grades 5 through 12 will enjoy the information about the invention and development of alphabets.

Works Cited

Crystal, D. *Spell It Out: The Curious, Enthralling, and Extraordinary Story of English Spelling*. New York: St. Martin's Press, 2009. Print.

Finegan, E. *Language: Its Structure and Uses*. 7th edition. New York: Wadsworth, 2014. Print.

Man, D. *Alpha Beta: How 26 Letters Shaped the Western World*. New York: John Wiley & Sons, 2000. Print.

Reutzel, D. R. and R. B. Cooter. *The Essentials of Teaching Children to Read: The Teacher Makes the Difference*. Boston: Pearson, 2013. Print.

Robb, D. *Ox, House, Stick: The History of Our Alphabet*. Watertown, MA: Charlesbridge, 2007. Print.

Sacks, D. *Language Visible: Unraveling the Mystery of the Alphabet from A to Z*. New York: Broadway, 2003. Print.

Sacks, D. *Letter Perfect: The Marvelous History of our Alphabet from A to Z*. New York: Broadway, 2003. Print.

Sacks, D. *The Alphabet*. New York: Broadway, 2003. Print.

Chapter 2

History of Alphabet Books

Once you learn to read, you will be forever free.
Frederick Douglass

Hornbooks

First published in the early 1600s in colonial times, alphabet books are recognized as one of the oldest genres available for children in America (Smolkin and Yaden 1992). They were adapted from the "hornbooks" or "lesson books" that had been printed in Europe in the 1450s. A hornbook is composed of a piece of parchment or paper pasted to a wooden board and protected by a very thin, see-through sheet of animal horn. The Puritans brought these hornbooks to America, using them as a way to teach their strong sense of values and morals. The alphabet was added to these religious books in the early 1600s, and "the purpose of these early primers was to instruct children in moral and religious beliefs, while letters were learned" (Cooper, p. 1). Hornbooks typically did not possess illustrations. Please see figure 2.1, "Wood Hornbook."

Battledores

Battledores replaced hornbooks in the mid-1700s, as their design created a more complex book. Their name is thought to have originated from the

Figure 2.1 Wood Hornbook, 18th Century. Courtesy of Rare Book and Special Collection of the Library of Congress

Figure 2.2   American Cardboard Battledore. Courtesy of Rare Book and Special Collection of the Library of Congress

resemblance of the battledore book in size and shape to the wooden racquet used in the game of battledore, a colonial version of badminton. Words were printed on thin cardboard, often folded into thirds, with accompanying illustrations that added to the entertaining aspect of these books. Although these books reflected current sociocultural and religious ideas as well as teaching the alphabet, battledores revealed a gradual shift toward more secular topics. They were published until the end of the 19th century. Please see figure 2.2, "American Cardboard Battledore."

Primers

During the middle of the 1800s, little books of multiple pages covered by a thick, protective binding became popular for children. The purpose of these little books, or primers,

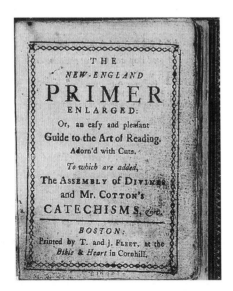

Figure 2.3   *The New England Primer* (title page). Courtesy of Rare Book and Special Collection of the Library of Congress

Figure 2.4   *The New England Primer* (inside page). Courtesy of Rare Book and Special Collection of the Library of Congress

was to teach the alphabet through letter–picture associations; religious objects were the primary subject matter. Printed and used mainly by churches, primers became the mainstay for reading instruction until the early 1900s.

The New England Primer

Originally published in 1777, *The New England Primer* was the first beginner reader primer published in the American colonies. It became the most successful book for teaching children to read until the 1800s and was still used until 1900. Although it included the alphabet in rhyme form, its primary purpose was religious instruction. Please see figures 2.3, *"The New England Primer* (title page),*"* and 2.4, *"The New England Primer* (inside page).*"*

Connections from Past to Present

Abecedarius

An abecedarius is a "26-line rhymed verse that uses successive letters of the alphabet at the beginning of each line" (Cooper, p. 85). For centuries, this poetic format served as the template for teaching the alphabet and was portrayed in colonial primers and alphabet cards. As evidenced in *The Ladder to Learning* (1852) by Miss Lovechild ("A stands for ape, for Arthur, for air, B stands for bullock, for bird, and for bear"), the abecedarius appeared frequently in alphabet books of the 19th and 20th centuries, and it still brightens the pages of contemporary alphabet books.

Two Journeys of "A Apple Pie" Abecedariuses

A nursery rhyme, sung by English children in the 1600s while playing, became the connection for three alphabet books over the next four centuries. Originally published in 1886, Kate Greenaway's charming book *A Apple Pie: An Old Fashioned Alphabet Book* portrayed this playful rhyme. Her work was recreated by Watchmaker Publishing in 2012, including the same text and bold, full-page, color illustrations.

Nearly four centuries later and connecting to the same English nursery rhyme, Gennady Spirin created another charming and delightful portrayal of the alphabet, *A Apple Pie* (2005). Bringing to life this alphabet rhyme about the enjoyment of an apple pie, with "A apple pie, B bit it, C cut it, D dealt it," and so on, Spirin presents the capital and lowercase letters in both cursive and manuscript printing.

In a similar fashion, Alison Murray (*Apple Pie ABC*, 2012) builds upon the "A Apple Pie" lines but adds a playful puppy to share in the pie's enjoyment. In this joyful tale of "Apple Pie, Bake it, Cool it, Dish it out," connections to the original playful song can be heard.

For the second "A Apple Pie" abecedarius journey, Edward Lear penned his famous alphabet poem entitled "A Apple Pie," which appeared in the 1871 book *Nonsense Songs, Stories, Botany, and Alphabets.* Lear encouraged and applauded literary nonsense with this rhyming ditty: "A was once an apple pie, Pidy, Widy, Tidy, Pidy, Nice insidy, Apple Pie!" But note that his text, although rhyming and using words in alphabetical order, is not consistent with the original nursery rhyme of the 1600s.

In 2005, illustrator and author Suse MacDonald adapted Edward Lear's classic alphabet rhyme and enhanced his "A Apple Pie" alphabet poem, describing more options for the pie and providing vibrant watercolor illustrations. Entitled *Edward Lear's A Was Once an Apple Pie* (2005), Macdonald's delightful book sings with language play and childhood happiness.

The Shaker Abecedarius

Almost hidden within other lines of black and white text, the Shaker abecedarius, created by an unnamed father for his many children, was published in the *Shaker Manifesto* (1882). This brief poem listed only twenty-four letters of the alphabet and used animal names to represent each beginning sound. Almost 100 years later, Alice and Martin Provensen borrowed the original Shaker abecedarius and expanded it, both in letters and in colorful watercolor illustrations for which the Provensens were known and admired. Their much-loved classic alphabet book, *A Peaceable Kingdom: A Shaker Abecedarius* (1978), shows the interplay between the Shakers' strictly disciplined lifestyle and their love of rhyme, music, and dance. Over 100 animals are named in this rhyming poem, and illustrations depict typical colonial clothing and daily activities. Created with the idea that children would enjoy lighthearted rhymes about animals, this alphabet book presented a less serious tone than earlier ABC books.

Acrobatic Alphabets

Unique to the genre of alphabet books is the concept of "posture master" alphabets. This concept of using human bodies, either through illustrations or actual living beings, to form the letters of the alphabet has connections through the centuries. Various primers in the 1700s and early 1800s utilized posture master alphabets as their educational format. In addition to alphabet books, alphabet cards were used during the colonial period for educational purposes. These alphabet letters were drawn as human figures positioning their bodies in the shapes of the letters. In 1782, a twenty-four letter alphabet (without J and U) was published by Carington Bowles and served as the foundation for these entertaining alphabet cards (The Colonial Williamsburg Foundation). Various primers in the 1700s and early 1800s also utilized posture master alphabets as their educational format. Connecting this unique letter depiction over the span of two centuries are two recent alphabet books, *D is for Drums: A Colonial Williamsburg ABC* (2004) and *The Human Alphabet* (2005). Within Kay Chorao's charming book about colonial life, *D is for Drums: A Colonial Williamsburg ABC*, hand-drawn human figures twist and link hands to form each of the 26 letters. In their extraordinary book, *The Human Alphabet*, the dance company Philobus created each letter and an accompanying object that begins with the featured letter using two or more dancers.

ABC Books of Today

Baby board books, interactive books with tactile features, three-dimensional books, bilingual books, and electronic books now constitute the vast array of modern alphabet books. Alphabet books appear on every topic and appeal to all ages and grades. For beginning readers, alphabet books that teach the sequence of the alphabet, focusing on the shape and sound of each letter, abound in schools and libraries. Themed alphabet books about science, social studies, and multiculturalism present engaging facts about concepts and provide interesting formats to delineate those concepts into 26 interlocking pieces of factual information.

The role of the illustrator in alphabet books, as in all genres of children's books, has become more important. One of the many joys of children's literature are the illustrations. Illustrations connect readers more deeply to the written word as well as open their eyes to new ways of seeing the world. "Artists have adopted the genre as a playground for plying their imaginative works" (Cooper, p. 2). All of the medium possibilities (acrylic or oil paint, collage, gouache, pen and ink, photography, sculpture, and watercolor, for instance) are explored and included in contemporary alphabet books. Within the last three decades, seven alphabet books have been recognized for their outstanding illustrations by receiving a Caldecott Honor Book Award. "What began as a simple reader for children has evolved into an appealing collection of illustrations, text, and information that is also fascinating" (Cooper, p. 2).

Five publishing companies shine in both quantity and quality of recent publications of alphabet books. Each one possesses a unique, inviting perspective on alphabet books.

Abdo Publishers (www.abdopublishing.com)

Abdo Publishers created two alphabet book series, *Let's See A thru Z* and *Let's Look A thru Z*. With a user-friendly and informative Web site, Abdo Publishers provides teachers with a wealth of instructional books and additional curricular resources.

(continued)

(*continued*)

Charlesbridge Publishing Company (www.charlesbridge.com)

Housing the myriad alphabet books by famed science author Jerry Pallotta, this publishing company also presents a few bilingual alphabet books. Other topics, such as *ABC Book of American Homes*, are part of the books published by the prolific Charlesbridge.

Chronicle Publishing Company (www.chroniclebooks.com)

This colorful, engaging Web site houses Chronicle Publishing Company, well known for its alphabet books and other teacher resources, such as alphabet flash cards, blocks, and notes. Among its recent titles are *Abraham: A Jewish Family Alphabet* and *T Is for Tugboat: Navigating the Seas from A to Z*.

Sleeping Bear Press (www.sleepingbearpress.com)

Sleeping Bear Press, an internationally recognized publisher of children's books, has published 51 titles about each of the U.S. states, plus Washington, D.C., as a series entitled *Discover America State by State*. A teacher's guide for this state series by a well-known educator, Eugene Gagliano, is presented on its engaging Web site. In addition to its state series, Sleeping Bear Press has published over 100 topics as alphabet books for middle and secondary classrooms.

The Quatro Group (www.quartoknows.com)

Publishing the growing series of currently 24 *World Alphabet* books, this company's alphabet books include *E Is for Ethiopia, I Is for Israel,* and *M Is for Mexico*. By providing bold photographs and informative texts about the people and cultures of countries of the world, these *World Alphabet* books are wonderful assets for the multicultural curriculum.

The first children's bookstore in America opened in Boston in 1916. For 100 years, parents and educators have been able to purchase books especially written for children!

Librarians' Link

Librarians will enjoy knowing that it was in the 1830s that the first public libraries opened in the United States. By the end of the 1800s, people in all parts of the world could peruse and borrow books from public libraries within their local communities. Currently, most libraries are connected electronically to enable their patrons to discover an ever-increasing supply of books and other digital materials (*Scholastic Voyages of Discovery*).

Listed below are useful and interesting Web Sites about the history of alphabet books for librarians to share with teachers and students.

Notable Web Sites

http://rarebookschool.org/2005/exhibitions.dickandjane.shtml

This engaging Web site offers a charming history of the influential Dick and Jane primers that were published in 1930 and shaped beginning reading instruction for 30 years. Samples of the text and colorful pictures of the classic characters enhance this pleasant and informative Web site.

http://content.lib.washington.edu

Nestled within the intriguing text about the historical development of children's books are several examples of hornbooks, battledores, and primers, and a collection of early American alphabet books. This amazing Web site offers detailed information and excellent color photos.

http://www.stellabooks.com/article/abc-a-history-of-alphabet-books

Providing an interesting, informative history of alphabet books, this article discusses hornbooks, primers, and other books in the evolution of alphabet books. Sharing examples of alphabet books as they developed over time, this article also includes insights about the importance of alphabet books as a teaching tool.

Works Cited

The Colonial Williamsburg Foundation. Williamsburg, VA: n.p., 1995. Print.

Cooper, C. H. *ABC Books and Activities from Preschool to High School.* Lanham, MD: The Scarecrow Press, 1996. Print.

Scholastic Voyages of Discovery. Editions: Gallimard Jeunesse, 1995. Print.

Smolkin, L. B., and D. B. Yaden Jr. "O Is for Mouse: First Encounters with the Alphabet Book." *Language Arts* 69 (1992): 432–41. Print.

Chapter 3

Teaching with Alphabet Books

All words are pegs to hang ideas on.
Henry Ward Beecher

Instructional Value of Alphabet Books

For several decades, teachers of all grades have enjoyed the various benefits of using alphabet books within their classrooms. Although alphabet books are traditionally considered as only appropriate for elementary grades, innovative and creative teachers of middle and secondary students have effectively used these books to enhance the curriculum in very engaging, interesting ways.

Alphabet Books and Younger Students

The primary purpose of alphabet books for young children is to learn the alphabet and "to associate a specific letter with objects that have that particular initial letter" (Kormanski and Stevens, p. 55). In addition to learning the alphabet, young children also begin their exploration of wordplay, hearing the rhyme and rhythm of language, discovering the similar sounds of alliteration, and expanding their vocabularies through funny, fanciful words not usually seen in beginner reader books. Reading and rereading alphabet books to very young children provides oral language development. Preschoolers and early readers learn various concepts of print (authors, turning pages, directionality of print, and other book usage aspects) from handling and exploring alphabet books (Warner and Weiss).

Alphabet Books and Older Students

Teachers of middle and secondary students have discovered a recent upsurge in the number and quality of alphabet books appropriate for use in their classrooms. For older students, alphabet books provide expository information to supplement their textbooks in different content areas, especially the sciences. In particular, Sleeping Bear Press and Charlesbridge Publishing Company have published, within the last several years, over 200 titles of alphabet books that contain both advanced vocabulary terms and discussions of conceptual topics. Under Charlesbridge Publishing, Jerry Pallotta, has published over 40 alphabet books about life science and earth science topics. Pallotta's alphabet books, along with those of other authors, present facts in enjoyable, interesting formats. Science alphabet books engage reluctant readers and "serve as a perfect tool for differentiating instruction for students with diverse needs" (Bromley np). Less able readers will enjoy the charming rhymes, while more advanced readers can gain in-depth knowledge through a detailed explanation of historical and scientific facts.

Alphabet books can be used also as engaging supplementary texts in the social studies area. Sleeping Bear Press has published 51 titles about each of the U.S. states, plus Washington, D.C., as a series entitled *Discover America State by State*. In addition to their state series, Sleeping Bear Press has published over 100 topics as alphabet books for middle-schoolers. Such titles as *D Is for Drinking Gourd* (an African American history), *T Is for Time*, and *I Is for Idea* portray complex topics within the social studies domain.

Alphabet Books as Mentor Texts

With the surge of alphabet books that focus on conceptual topics and use the alphabet letters as conduits to provide expository information in an engaging format, teachers can choose from a variety of high-quality books on several content topics. History alphabet books describe the American Revolutionary War, leaders Abraham Lincoln and Benjamin Franklin, and patriotic and civic responsibilities of living in a democracy. Within the fields of mathematics, world history, and geography, alphabet books display conceptual knowledge with vibrant illustrations and energetic vocabularies that engage secondary readers. Evers, Lang, and Smith included content alphabet books within a writing workshop curriculum and used the books "as anchor texts for a literacy journey across all content areas" (p. 462). Incorporating alphabet books within the content area curricula provides models for students to generate their own ABC books about topics of interest; for example, *The ABCs of Fractions* or *The Alphabet Book about Matter and Energy* (Bromley np).

The instructional uses and benefits of alphabet books within all classroom grades are limitless. While acknowledging that excellent teachers can connect curricular standards to almost any text, a comprehensive review of the list of alphabet books in chapter 5 highlights the following instructional values that these books provide.

Language Arts

Language arts supplies the foundation for creating excellent and essential curricula. Learning to read and comprehend various kinds of text is the number one predictor of school success (Reutzel and Cooter). The six subsets of the language arts domain are reading, writing, speaking, listening, viewing, and visually representing (Tompkins).

Alliteration

Integral to any language arts program is the teaching of alliteration, or the repetition of the beginning sound of words in sequence. By hearing and recognizing these beginning sounds, students are engaging in phonological awareness (Pitcher and Mackey; Reutzel and Cooter; Tompkins). In addition to emphasizing sounds of language for younger students, alphabet books that utilize alliteration serve as excellent mentor texts for instructional purposes when teaching this writing technique to older students.

- *Animalia* (1993) by Graeme Base contains clever, colorful descriptions of animals in alliterative phrases, such as "an armoured armadillo avoiding an angry alligator" and "beautiful blue butterflies basking by a babbling brook."
- In a similar fashion, author Tad Hill creates exciting word pictures of everyday objects in *R Is for Rocket: An ABC Book* (2015). Descriptions such as "Bella bounces on a ball while a big, blue butterfly watches" delight readers with the repetitive sounds of language play.
- Author Crescent Dragonwagon employs alliteration in her charming book entitled *All the Awake Animals Are Almost Asleep* (2012) with colorful phrases such as "Cat's curled up on a crimson couch cushion."
- One interesting aspect of alliteration involves creating an alliterative sentence or phrase in which the last word begins with the letter for the following page. Nicholas Heller's *Ogres! Ogres! Ogres!: A Feasting Frenzy from A to Z* (1999) employs this technique throughout the book. For example, with "Melanie merrily munches nuts, and Nicodemus nibbles numerous oysters," Heller entices the reader with a subtle hint of alphabetical foreshadowing.

Alphabetic Principle

In 2016, virtually all reading educators espouse the value of teaching the alphabetic principle to beginning readers (National Reading Panel). Learning the alphabetic principle involves the understanding that specific letters or letter combinations represent specific sounds. For example, in the English alphabet, the letter M represents the /m/ sound. When children are able to combine their phonological awareness (sounds of language) with written letter-name knowledge, they have mastered the alphabetic principle. Mastering the alphabetic principle is "absolutely necessary for almost all students to make progress in their reading development" (Reutzel and Cooter, p. 92).

Alphabet books, especially those in the single letter category, provide an excellent avenue for learning the alphabetic principle. Displaying a single large letter (either capital or lowercase) on each page in alphabetical order and the accompanying object that begins with that letter helps students to name and remember that letter.

- An excellent book that highlights the correspondence between written letters and their sounds is Suse MacDonald's *Alphabatics* (1986). The boldly colored, lowercase letters transform to become objects that begin with the same letters. By including a clear, concise image of a single object, accompanied by the word, MacDonald connects the letter with its sound, creating engaging, acrobatic depictions of the alphabetical principle.

- Donna Maurer's *Annie, Bea, and Chi Chi Dolores: A School Day Alphabet* (1993) presents in wonderful fashion all those fun activities children do at schools. The large, bold capital and lowercase letters describe one event per letter, with C for counting, D for drawing, H for hopping, and G for giggling.
- Flora McDonnell's *ABC* (1997) explodes with one huge animal and bold capital and lowercase letters on each page. Depicting an exemplary simplicity of the alphabetic principle for emerging readers, McDonnell engages with a newt (and a newspaper) and an orangutan (and an orange).
- Clement Hurd's thoughtful alphabet book that describes those memorable items in Margaret Wise Brown's classic children's story reinforces the alphabetic principle. In *Goodnight Moon ABC: An Alphabet Book* (2010), A is for air and H is for house—and children everywhere can connect these cherished items from Brown's *Goodnight Moon* to the written alphabet.

Descriptive Writing

Alphabet books can be used as excellent examples for writing mini-lessons stressing alliteration, rhyme, and precise, concise word choice. Alphabet books can also use the framework of the alphabet as a device to organize creative writing around a particular topic, utilizing content vocabulary.

- Roy Blount Jr.'s *Alphabet Juice* (2008) and *Alpha Better Juice* (2011) describe selected enigmatic terms in a dictionary format. Students in grades 7–12 will value this alphabet book as a helpful resource and an enlightening guide for very unusual words.
- Chelsey McLaren and Pamela Jaber depict nonfictional information about clothes and clothing styles in their very colorful, clever book, *When Royals Wore Ruffles: Funny and Fashionable Alphabet!* (2009). By using a descriptive, humorous vocabulary, the authors show the value of word choice to create engaging informative text.
- The literary format of short stories shines in *Once Upon an Alphabet: Short Stories for All the Letters* (2014) by Oliver Jeffers. Each letter describes a humorous or insightful idea captured with imagination and an abundance of dialogue. Thus, this alphabet book serves as an exemplary model for writing techniques.
- In *What I Hate from A to Z*, author Roz Chast (2011) utilizes a graphic novel format as part of the book's organizational structure and thus presents an excellent instructional model of this writing style for upper elementary and secondary students.

Grammar

"A rule system, or grammar, governs all languages. The English language is essentially based on a subject-verb grammar system" (Reutzel and Cooter, p. 111). Alphabet books that teach components of grammar provide fun and (usually) funny examples of sometimes tedious grammar rules. These cleverly written books engage students and serve as excellent supplementary resources for teaching grammar.

- *Antics* by Cathi Hepworth (1992) is a clever book that uses the word "ant" within the descriptions of 26 objects. What a unique, interesting way to present prefixes and suffixes, along with root words.
- In *AlphaBest: The Zany, Zanier, and Zaniest Book about Comparatives and Superlatives* (2012), Helaine Becker presents an entertaining way to teach about adjectives, comparatives, and superlatives. Her helpful book even includes a teaching guide.
- Colleen Dolphin created a worthy book about adjectives in *Adventurous to Zealous: All About Me from A to Z* (2009). Every page depicts a letter and several adjectives (such as "independent" and "imaginative" for the letter I) beginning with that letter and also includes a sentence using one of the words.
- *F Is for Feeling* (2014) by Goldie Millar and Lisa Berger provides a helpful mentor text for teaching adjectives. Twenty-six letters of the alphabet form the foundation to describe human feelings, such as "D is for Determined. I'm trying hard and I think I can do it."

Phonemic Awareness

Reading experts advocate the simultaneous teaching of both the alphabetic principle and phonemic awareness for beginning reading instruction (Clay; Reutzel and Cooter). Not only is it important for children to recognize the relationship between written letters and sounds, but it is also essential for emerging readers to hear, say, and play with the sounds of language (Pitcher and Mackey). Within the pages of several alphabet books, words tumble and sounds rumble. It is the fascination with and enjoyment of the sounds of language that build the foundation for good readers.

- In Gyo Fujikawa's *A to Z Picture Book* (2010), several pictures fill two pages, reinforcing that particular beginning sound. For the letter B, blackberries, basket, bicycle, butterfly and many other smaller and larger pictures of /b/ words allow for repetition and practice in hearing and saying that phoneme.
- Daron Parton uses uncluttered alliteration in her book *Alligator in an Anorak* (2014). With engagingly sweet simplicity, she plays with language sounds in phrases such as "lion in the letterbox and mole in the middle."
- *My Sound Parade* (2001) by Jane Belk Moncure epitomizes the values of phonemic awareness, as each page displays language sounds. For example, the sentence "Little c rides a camel with a cat and a clown" reinforces the hard C, or /k/, sound.
- In *Augie to Zebra: An Alphabet Book!* (2012), author Casper Babypants describes 26 beautiful names from diverse cultures and places, for example, "Eliza educates the elephant." Each letter has an accompanying sentence and a picture that is full of phonic illustrations of that letter.

- Classic children's author Margaret Wise Brown creates language sounds for each letter in her book *Sleepy ABC* (2009). Wonderful pages of sounds, such as "A is for Aaaah when a small kitten sighs," softly sing children to sleep.

Rhyme and Rhythm

Like music, language has its rhymes and rhythms. Language play is often encouraged for preschoolers, as the sounds and cadences of words breathe life into reading and writing. From clapping syllables to creating rhyming word families, emergent readers who experience and participate in the nuances of oral language become the fluent readers and writers in upper elementary classrooms (Pitcher and Mackey).

- Within Joseph Slates' endearing book *Miss Bindergarten Gets Ready for Kindergarten* (1996), rhyming sentences enchant any child about the joys of kindergarten. Although the illustrations show animals in school, it is obvious that children will adore the playful rhymes, such as "Gwen McGunny packs her bunny. Henry Fetter fights his sweater."
- A wonderful book for teaching many kinds of poetry is Judy Young's *R Is for Rhyme: A Poetry Alphabet* (2005). This colorful, exciting book describes many kinds of poetry, including a rhyme pattern for each poem, and gives a beautiful example of that poetic structure. Poetry formats, such as the acrostic, the ballad, and the cinquain (to name a few), are explained with precise detail and much love.
- *Take Away the A* by Michaël Escoffier (2014) is an excellent book that teaches rhyming in a fun fashion. Cute, colorful illustrations accompany phrases such as, "Without the L the plants wear pants."
- In David and Zora Aiken's *All About Boats A to Z* (2012), four-lined, rhyming nautical poems splash onto the pages. Perfect for the early grades, the rhymes employ easily recognizable words (sight words or high frequency words).

Vocabulary

Vocabulary allows ideas, stories, and life experiences to be spoken, heard, written, and read for understanding. It is difficult to overestimate the importance of vocabulary for reading success and ultimately school success. Children who come to school knowing thousands of words through oral language and read-alouds have a tremendous advantage over those children who have limited vocabulary or a language-deprived background (Johnson; Lervag and Auhrust; National Reading Panel).

Vocabulary and Younger Students

In beginner alphabet books, quite often there is little text. The emphasis is on the association between the single letter and objects that begin with that letter. Word choice is thus crucial, and uncommon words (for six-year-olds!) are used frequently to capture that letter–object connection.

- In *Fancy Nancy's Favorite Fancy Words: From Accessories to Zany* (2008), author Jane O'Connor adds exciting, entertaining words like "accessories," "boa." and "ooh la la." The vocabulary sometimes includes French words.
- Likewise, children will be delighted with the swashbuckling word choices, such as "buccaneer" and "plundering," about pirates in Caroline Still's *An ABC of Pirates* (2010). The cartoon format will appeal to reluctant readers.
- In *M Is for Music* (2003), Kathleen Krull broadens our musical vocabulary with 26 terms, including a paragraph description of each. A glossary at the end of the book reinforces these musical concepts.

Vocabulary and Older Students

Vocabulary remains paramount in middle and secondary grades, as conceptual knowledge becomes the core of the curriculum (Cunningham; Harmon et al.). "ABC books engage students in productive, fun, independent word learning across grade levels and content areas" (Bromley np). The following books are excellent resources for middle school and secondary classrooms.

- In *L Is for Lollygag: Quirky Words for a Clever Tongue* (2008), Tracy Sunrize Johnson describes clever and enigmatic words in a playful, conversational tone. This youthful presentation will make vocabulary learning enjoyable.
- *The Ultimate Alphabet* (1986) depicts 8,000 words through detailed paintings. For example, Mike Wilks presents over 360 words for the letter A. Students will be amazed at his mammoth array of vocabulary.

Specialized Languages in Alphabet Books

In addition to conventional alphabet books that employ twenty-six letters, two alphabet books explore specialized languages. These specialized languages offer intriguing ways to view language communication via visual and code formats.

- In *The Handmade Alphabet* (1991), author Laura Rankin depicts hand positions in American Sign Language, with a corresponding written word and object. Teachers of very young children and children with special needs will find this book helpful in their classrooms.
- In Chris Demarest's exciting book about the military entitled *Alpha, Bravo, Charlie: The Military Alphabet* (2005), two forms of communication are presented. These communication codes include the U.S. Navy signal flags (where each flag represents a letter) and the International Communication Association alphabet (where a word represents a letter).

Mathematics

Some educators place as much, if not more, emphasis upon the content area of mathematics as they do on language arts. Mathematics encompasses number concepts that tell how much or how many, with the accompanying numerals or words that represent numbers. Also within this content area lie numeral operations, measurement, geometric shapes, and concepts. Within the last decade, a wealth of alphabet books about mathematics has entranced teachers and students with their sharp, concise vocabulary and enjoyable illustrations.

- Colleen Dolphin's engaging book *Angles to Zeros: Mathematics from A to Z* (2008) describes 26 mathematical concepts, using definitions and illustrations easily recognized by students. With D for diameter, a picture of a pie being cut in half is portrayed. For "fraction," representing the letter F, six lanes in a swimming pool are shown, with an explanation of each lane equaling one-sixth of the pool. A glossary and "More Math" sections at the end of the book encourage and inspire students' content vocabulary and deeper research into those topics of interest.

Geometry and Measurement

- In David Schwartz's *G Is for Googol: A Math Alphabet Book* (1998), terms such as "B is for binary" and "P is for probability" are presented with a sense of amazement and enjoyment. Students who are math phobic will delight in the clever, sometimes humorous descriptions of complicated mathematical concepts. Illustrations of a graphic novel format add to the appeal of this engaging alphabet book.
- Ann Whitford Paul's story of quilting, *Eight Hands Round: A Patchwork Alphabet* (1996), serves as a real life utilization of geometry concepts. With each letter describing a specific geometric quilt pattern—for example, M is for maple leaf pattern—each page displays a quilt pattern at the bottom.

Number and Operations

- In Elisha Cooper's delightful book about animals, *8: An Animal Alphabet* (2015), animal names are presented in alphabetical order. Numbering and counting are emphasized, as each page asks readers to find eight occurrences of a specific animal.
- John Nickle's *Alphabet Explosion! Search and Count from Alien to Zebra* (2006) challenges students to find a specific number of objects that begin with a specific letter; for example, "Find 22 objects that begin with the letter A." For students who love searching for items hidden within illustrations, this unique book will provide hours of fun.
- *26 Letters and 99 Cents* (1995), by Tana Hoban, presents bold, bright numerals with their matching values in pennies, nickels, dimes, and quarters. On the flip side of the book, each bold, bright letter is matched with an everyday object that begins with that letter. This cheerful book will delight young children who are learning the letters and numerals.

- Nick Bruel continues his series with poor Puppy and bad Kitty while teaching letters and numerals to young readers. In his *Poor Puppy and Bad Kitty* (2012), Puppy finds 1 airplane, 2 balls, and 24 other items in alphabetical order to amuse himself while Kitty takes a nap.

Science

Four branches within the science curricula include chemical, earth, life, and physical sciences. Several alphabet books provide students of all grade levels opportunities to explore their environment, to read interesting facts about plants and animals, and to discover how things work. The scientific process of developing a hypothesis, collecting data, and finding results comes to life in engaging alphabet books.

- As a tribute to the inquisitive spirit of scientists, Larry Verstraete's remarkable book *S Is for Scientists: A Discovery Alphabet* (2010) captures the excitement and challenge of generating new knowledge through adapting, building, comparing, and demonstrating (to name a few of the 26 scientist qualities). This amazing book will inspire and motivate budding scientists.
- Brimming with scientific knowledge, *Q Is for Quark: A Science Alphabet Book* (2001), by David Schwartz, highlights 26 concepts with thorough definitions and realistic illustrations. Topics, such as DNA, gravity, the immune system, and Y chromosomes, fill the pages of this wonderfully accessible science alphabet book.
- In George Shannon's *Tomorrow's Alphabet* (1996), an innovative and enlightening approach to teaching the concept of cause and effect is boldly portrayed with vivid, colorful images and few words; for example, "B is for eggs—tomorrow's Birds." This excellent book provokes thought in younger children as they begin to explore scientific investigations.

One of the excellent aspects of science alphabet books is "the inclusion of full color photographs and detailed drawings that provide readers with a sense of being on-site" (Cooper, p. 69). Many of the science alphabet books can be used to supplement the traditional science textbook. For elementary students, these books connect the alphabet to interesting facts about nature, animals, and weather (to name a few), while middle and secondary students see their value as "reference sources of information about birds, fish, flowers, and other aspects of nature; as examples of materials to examine for scientific accuracy; as models to describe relationships in nature; and as a means of investigating a scientific topic in an alphabetical sequence" (Cooper, p. 71).

Chemical Science

- As part of an exciting new science series entitled *Jumbo Minds' Science ABCs*, author Lemonwood presents chemistry terms and concepts in an alphabetical format. Featuring such topics as "Atom," "Bond," and "Zinc," *ABCs of Chemistry* (2015) defines and describes 26 basic chemistry terms, accompanying each with colorful, friendly illustrations.

Earth Science

- John Farrell captures the brilliance and aura of the night sky in his enjoyable book, *Stargazer's Alphabet: Night-Sky Wonders from A to Z* (2007). With beautiful photographs and interesting facts, this book describes the constellations Cygnus and Draco and other stargazer's delights.
- *Alphasaurs and Other Prehistoric Types* (2012), by Sharon Werner and Sarah Forss, features dinosaurs that are formed by the typefaces of the alphabet letters themselves. For an intriguing journey into geological and archaeological discoveries of ancient dinosaurs, this book will delight the budding scientist.
- In *Alphabet of Earth* (2011), Barbie Heit Schwaeber describes earth science items in four lines of rhyme. Accompanying one large, colorful capital and lowercase letter per page, the concept sings with a catchy rhyme. For example, "J is for Jungle. Reptiles, birds and insects are the jungle population. This green and leafy environment is brimming with vegetation."
- Amazing facts about the weather are discussed in *W Is for Wind: A Weather Alphabet* (2005), by Pat Michaels. For each of 26 weather topics, such as "B is for barometer," Michaels has created a four-line rhyming poem and included helpful scientific facts.
- Ruth Strother's informative alphabet book, *B Is for Blue Planet: An Earth Science Alphabet* (2011), depicts concepts about our blue planet. Presenting earth science vocabulary such as "coral reef" and "desert," this book excites and inspires the budding geologist.

Life Science

Jerry Pallotta's books are well known as tools to make science fun for students. With over 40 books about life science and earth science, Pallotta's series of alphabet books about ancient animals, cool critters, garden goodies, and enduring ecosystems engage and excite students of all ages. The realistic illustrations and enjoyable text form a winning combination for presenting and discussing scientific terms.

- In *The Flower Alphabet Book* (1989), Jerry Pallotta describes 26 gorgeous flowers, including facts about their growth, their uses, and the reasons for their names. Likewise, he depicts 26 creatures in the ocean, along with engaging facts, in *The Ocean Alphabet Book*.
- Andrew Zuckerman provides an animal clue with the beginning letter, and on the following page, a colorful, full-page illustration with the animal name is presented. More life science facts about each of the 26 animals are given in the glossary of his *Creature ABC* (2009).
- Mary Azarian creates lush natural scenes with classic gardening concepts and striking woodcut illustrations in *A Gardener's Alphabet* (2000). Simple in its text, the book sets the stage for emerging readers as they explore words like "arbor," "bulbs," and "compost."
- In *A Paddling of Ducks: Animals in Groups from A to Z* (2010), author Marjorie Blain Parker teaches collective nouns for animal groups in a delightful, charming way. Colorful illustrations add to the enjoyment of this wonderful life science book.

Physical Science

- As a part of the science series entitled *Jumbo Minds Science ABCs* (2015), *ABCs of Physics* contains 26 physics terms presented in an easy-to-understand format. Defining and discussing topics such as acceleration and buoyancy, A. C. Lemonwood engages the young reader with physical science concepts in everyday happenings.

Social Studies

The domain of social studies curricula includes the study of culture, geography, economics, politics, and historical events and leaders. An alphabet book with appropriate text that conveys conceptual knowledge about social studies provides students with a supplemental and often more engaging source for classroom instruction. "History and social studies texts especially are dense and include subject-specific vocabulary that students may not have the background to understand" (Pitcher and Mackey, p. 168). Through their bold, authentic illustrations or photographs, alphabet books paint historical pictures of the past and bold depictions of the present. "Many ABC books are useful to share historical information, point out important events and facts about the past, and trace the history and culture of a particular country, culture, lifestyle, or region" (Cooper, p. 83).

Culture

- Within the colorful pages of *B Is for Brooklyn* (2012*)*, author Selina Alko celebrates the diverse populations and colorful, unique sites that contribute to Brooklyn's culture. Capturing the local places, events, and food in one of New York City's well-known boroughs, the book brims with engaging, entertaining concepts about Brooklyn and serves as an excellent supplementary text to the social studies curriculum.
- Richard Michelson's *A Is for Abraham: A Jewish Family Alphabet* (2008) depicts customs, foods, and historical events that have shaped Jewish culture. From "B is for Bar and Bat Mitzvahs" to "C could be for challah, chicken soup, or Chanukah," this book depicts elements of Jewish culture with warmth and love.
- Michael Shoulders has created a truly unique book that describes 26 kinds of homes. Revealing the many ways and places that Americans call home, *The ABC Book of American Homes* (2008) instantly captures the reader's attention with its depiction of a houseboat, an igloo, a farmhouse, and other unusual dwellings.
- In *A–Z of the World Cup* (2014), Hurley brings to life the excitement, the culture, and the sportsmanship of soccer players competing for the World Cup. This book is sure to be a favorite of sports enthusiasts everywhere, as it discusses countries such as Brazil and China and their roles in the World Cup.

Geography

Intrinsic to the field of geography is the study of maps and the impact and influence of geographical regions upon local, state, national, and international laws and customs. From a kindergartener's crayon drawing of a compass rose to a senior's detailed, computerized map of Western European countries, geography, alongside history and culture, composes part of the social studies curriculum.

- In Munro's *Mazeways A to Z* (2007), aerial illustrations of an airport, a shipyard, and other places of interest capture the excitement of maps with real life views. The importance of geography becomes magnified in this informative book.

- Students can travel through Helen L. Wilbur's *B Is for Beacon: A Great Lakes Lighthouse Alphabet* (2016) and navigate the five Great Lakes in America. This book presents landmarks, maps, and nautical concepts in colorfully illustrated pages.

- In a book swelling with country charm, Arthur Geisert describes farm concepts with simplicity and encompassing illustrations. Students can feel the nostalgia of a bygone era in *Country Road ABC: An Illustrated Journey through America's Farmland* (2010).

- Important geographical places are depicted in *Alcatraz to Zanzibar: Famous Places from A to Z* (2009). Author Colleen Dolphin includes interesting items, such as the Empire State Building and Zanzibar, to capture students' attention.

History

The field of history comprises the accumulation of recorded data involving leaders, communities, countries, events, and locations. Historians recognize that generations build upon the past and that civilizations everywhere evolve and transition to the beat of time's endless march.

- Alan Schroeder has created an endearing yet informative book about one of America's most noted leaders. In *Abe Lincoln: His Wit and Wisdom from A–Z* (2015), Schroeder's cartoon-like illustrations and his friendly depiction of Lincoln will thrill even the most reluctant history student.
- Beaming with American patriotism and pride, Wendell Minor's *Yankee Doodle America: The Spirit of 1776 from A to Z* (2006) represents the American Revolution of 1776, a classic American history lesson. Using hand-painted replicas of tavern signs, Minor captures the spirit that founded America. Two examples of tavern sign replicas include "A is for Acts" and "D is for Declaration."
- Nancy Sanders describes customs and historical events that impacted the African American heritage in *D Is for Drinking Gourd: An African American Alphabet* (2007). The book ends with a selected reference list of similar topics.

- *N Is for Our Nation's Capital: A Washington DC Alphabet* (2005), written by Marie and Roland Smith, depicts the history of this city through both text and watercolor illustrations of monuments and historical events. This informative, enjoyable book is part of the *Discover America State by State* series as the 51st volume!

Fine Arts

Students can explore art images and graphic design through cleverly designed alphabet books. Different media are presented, including acrylic or oil paint, collage, gouache, pen and ink, photography, sculpture, and watercolor. The illustrations in alphabet books serve as excellent examples of artistic expression and challenge students to develop their visual literacy through understanding the ideas conveyed in graphic design and by refining their observations and perceptions.

Graphic Design

Also known as communication design, graphic design involves creatively portraying ideas and experiences using visual and textual content. As beautifully displayed in the following alphabet books, graphic design can be enjoyed over time and repeatedly. The reader has the control over the pace and the sequence of these visual experiences.

- Woop Studios employs vivid digital images of groups of animals in the enticing book, *Zeal of Zebras* (2011). While also teaching collective nouns, such as "a caravan of camels," this book reminds us of the power of visual communication.
- *All Aboard!: A Traveling Alphabet* (2008), by Bill Mayer, uses mixed media images to create large, bold, and colorful graphics associated with the 26 letters. He adds an accompanying word, such as "*BRIDGE*" for the letter B, in a slanted position to indicate speed.
- Within the colorful pages of *Beautiful Birds* (2015), Jean Roussen creates detailed images of 26 birds with digital perfection. "C is for crane, both whooping and crowned" serves as an example of the lyrical text.

Observations and Perceptions

Students rely on personal observations and perceptions to gain understanding and appreciation of art forms. Sensitivity to surroundings, life experiences, and visual images spark the reader's interactions with the illustrations in alphabet books.

- In *Gone Wild: An Endangered Alphabet Book* (2006), David Linemas presents striking black-and-white images of endangered animals, composed of their initial capital letters. These letter-animals grow feathers, have paws, and produce antlers.

- By rotating Lisa Campbell Ernst's *The Turn-Around, Upside-Down Alphabet Book* (2004) on all four sides, a bold capital letter can be perceived as several other objects. This interactive book challenges perceptions and invites the reader's imagination to soar.
- Leslie McGuirk's creative alphabet book presents rocks in the shapes of the 26 letters. Students will enjoy discovering items such as a rock in the shape of a bird, for the letter B, in *If Rocks Could Sing: A Discovered Alphabet* (2011).
- On each page of Suse MacDonald's *Alphabatics* (1986), a letter tilts and transforms through four boxes to create an item that begins with that letter. Using these illustrations to convey messages, her dynamic book cleverly plays with transforming shapes, such as the letter A tilting and turning to become an ark.

Librarians' Link

Author studies provide curricular connections and invigorate instruction. Encouraging students to review several books by the same author fosters interest in the author's life events and how they have shaped his or her writing topics and styles. By comparing and contrasting several books by the same author, students can recognize and differentiate various writing techniques and authors' use of literary devices, such as foreshadowing, onomatopoeia, similes, and metaphors. At the request of librarians or teachers, many authors will visit schools and discuss their books, their perseverance as budding authors, and their writing styles. To spark interest in enhancing instruction by adding an author study, the following Web sites provide exciting and educational information about authors who have created two or more alphabet books.

Notable Web Sites

Listed below are Web sites of several authors who have published two or more alphabet books.

www.aletheakontis.com
www.anita-lobel.com
www.audreywood.com
www.ayles.com
www.carolinestills.com
www.chrisdemarest.net
www.davidschwartz.com
www.jacketflap.com/alan-schroeder/3607
www.jerrypallotta.com
www.junesobel.com

www.mairakalman.com
www.richardmichelson.com
www.rolandsmith.com
www.samanthavamos.com
www.simonandschuster.com/authors/Giles-Andreae/
www.stephentjohnson.com
www.susemacdonald.com

Works Cited

Bromley, K. "ABC Books: Building Vocabulary and Engaging Students." International Reading Association, Chicago, 2010. Presentation.

Clay, M. *An Observation Survey of Early Literacy Achievement.* Portsmouth, NH: Heinemann, 1993. Print.

Cunningham, P. M. *What Really Matters in Vocabulary: Research-Based Practices Across the Curriculum.* New York: Pearson, 2009. Print.

Evers, A., L. Lang, and S. Smith. "An ABC Literacy Journey: Anchoring in Text, Bridging Language, and Creating Stories." *The Reading Teacher* 62 (6): 461–471. Print.

Harmon, J. M., K. D. Wood, and W. B. Hedrick. *Instructional Strategies for Teaching Content Vocabulary: Grades 4–12.* Newark, DE: International Reading Association, 2006. Print.

Kormanski, L. M., and C. B. Stevens. "Alphabet Books Can Be Used with Fluent Readers and Writers." *Reading Horizons* 34 (1) (1993): 54–61. Print.

National Reading Panel. *Teaching Children to Read: An Evidence-based Assessment of the Scientific Research Literature on Reading and Its Implications for Reading Instruction.* Washington, D.C.: National Institute of Child Health and Human Development, 2000. Print.

Pitcher, S., and B. Mackey. *Collaborating for Real Literacy: Librarian, Teacher, Literacy Coach and Principal.* 2nd edition. Santa Barbara, CA: ABC-CLIO, 2013. Print.

Reutzel, D. R., and R. B. Cooter Jr. *The Essentials of Teaching Children to Read: The Teacher Makes the Difference.* 3rd edition. Boston: Pearson, 2013. Print.

Tompkins, G. E. *Literacy for the 21st Century: A Balanced Approach.* 5th Ed. Upper Saddle River, NJ: Merrill/Prentice Hall, 2009. Print.

Warner, L., and S. Weiss. "Why Young Children Need Alphabet Books." *Kappa Delta Pi Record* 41 (3) (2005): 124–127. Print.

Chapter 4

Three Categories of Text Structures in Alphabet Books

Books are a uniquely portable magic.
Stephen King

What Is Text Structure?

"Text structure" refers to the many ways that an author can organize, or structure, the text of his or her book. Physical features of the text (such as chapter headings, paragraph organization, signal words, spacing, and visual inserts) are included within the text structure analysis (Reutzel and Cooter).

Alphabet books are a unique genre in picture books. By definition, alphabet books contain the 26 letters of the English alphabet, although these letters may be presented out of sequence, may be hidden within the illustrations, or may serve as visual cues for depicting varying levels of content complexity. "Typically, one-half to no more than two pages comprise the information for each letter. The page or pages may consist of the uppercase letter, the lowercase letter, or both accompanied by the featured word, the illustration, and the text. Most often limited to a 26-letter presentation, alphabet books rarely exceed 60 pages in length" (Chaney, p. 97).

During a review of over 300 alphabet books (summarized in chapter 5), three patterns of text structure of alphabet books emerged. These three text structures include (1) single letter, (2) hidden letters, and (3) conceptual text.

Single Letter

Within the text structure called "single letter," alphabet books share the following characteristics:

1. Clarity—simple, uncluttered pages with clear, easily read typeface

2. Single alphabet letter (capital, lowercase, or both)
3. Usually one or two objects per letter
4. Pictures of objects are easily identifiable
5. Text limited to only a few words

Alphabet books with the "single letter" text structure focus on teaching the alphabetic principle. Letters (either capital or lowercase, but usually both) are presented in a bold, clear fashion. Illustrations are uncluttered depictions of objects or people to which ordinary children already have a connection.

Single Letter Expanded

Due to the elaborate text of several alphabet books within the "single letter" category, the necessity of naming a subset of this category became obvious. Alphabet books that fit under the "single letter expanded" subcategory possess the defining characteristics of "single letter" books, with one exception—an extensive use of text. An excellent example of the "single letter expanded" category of text structure lies in the pages of *ABC Animal Jamboree* (2012) by Giles Andreae. Highlighting each alphabet letter with its corresponding animal, the text includes four or five lines of descriptive phrases per page. Likewise, in *Bang! Boom! Roar! A Busy Crew of Dinosaurs* (2012), Nate Evans describes dinosaurs at a construction site with four lines of rhyme per alphabet letter. Describing the lives of firefighters, Chris Demarest depicts twenty-six items by using two sentences of colorful rhyme in *Firefighters A to Z* (2000). In summary, those alphabet books using the "single letter" text structure that contain written phrases or sentences of more than a few words fall into the subset labeled "single letter expanded."

Highlighted Book with "Single Letter" Text Structure for Pre-K–Second Grade

For prekindergarten through 2nd-grade students, *Winnie-the-Pooh's ABC* (2004) represents all of the characteristics of the "single letter" text structure. With its careful depiction of both capital and lowercase letters on one page, accompanied by a single, uncluttered illustration of the word that begins with the designated letter, this book is designed to encourage students to connect the alphabet letters, in order, with items that have the same beginning sound. For the letter A, one brightly colored red apple appears, and for the letter B, a shiny, blue balloon floats upward in the sky. Both the apple and the balloon are easily identifiable objects in the everyday lives of children. The purpose of the "single letter" text structure is reinforced in this classic book. Learning the written letter-sound correspondence (alphabetic principle), enjoying the recognizable pictures, and hearing the repetition of language as the book is read and reread constitute the instructional values of *Winnie-the-Pooh's ABC*.

Instructional Activity with "Single Letter" Text Structure for Pre-K–Second Grade

Hands-on activities that reinforce the alphabetic principle provide memorable and effective ways to teach beginning letter sounds with accompanying objects. Within the English language, consonants possess usually only one sound associated with one letter, whereas vowels have at least two sounds per letter. Thus, consonants are taught first in most beginning reading programs.

Materials for Letter B Bear Activity
Brown bear template
Bows (can be used in hair, as bowtie, or elsewhere)
Belts
Buckles
Band-Aids (a favorite object for all children)
Boots
Rounded Popsicle sticks

After reading *Winnie-the-Pooh's ABC,* teachers hold up and name the B items of the activity, having students repeat the words. Students cut out the bear and glue B items onto the bear. Students also glue the letter B (capital and lowercase) onto the Popsicle stick or onto the boots of the bear. When finished, the students name all of the B items for the teacher. Teachers encourage conversations among children about other B items as they complete their activity. Oral language development fosters beginning reading skills. Please see figure 4.1 for a photograph of the completed activity.

Figure 4.1   Bear Bb

Highlighted Book with "Single Letter" Text Structure for Grades 3–6

Welcome to the wonderful world of marvelous, miniature people and things! In Valorie Fisher's *Ellsworth's Extraordinary*

Electric Ears and Other Amazing Alphabet Anecdotes (2003), each capital letter begins a clever, alliterative sentence. Letters are presented in alphabetical sequence and serve as the cue for several words that begin with that letter, in both the one-sentence text and the adorable, unique photographs of miniature toys, animals, objects, and people. Sentences such as "Alistair had an alarming appetite for acrobats" and "Betty believed in a big but balanced breakfast" are excellent examples of the "single letter" text structure. The book concludes with an alphabetical listing of objects to be discovered on each page.

Instructional Activity with "Single Letter" Text Structure for Grades 3–6

The hands-on activity includes both mathematics and language arts. Household items and miniature objects will be included in the scene for an authentic, creative project. This mathematics and language arts activity reinforces geometric shapes, symmetry, sentence structure, alliteration, and precise vocabulary.

Materials for Alphabet Miniature Scene
Tic Tacs or other small candies
Miniature marshmallows
Toothpicks
Miniature trucks and cars
Miniature people
Miniature animals and other items
Variety of art supplies (glue, markers, paints)
Card stock for floor and background of miniature scene

Students will draw, from a hat or a bag, a letter of the alphabet. Each student will design and create three geometric shapes using Tic Tacs, miniature marshmallows, toothpicks, etc. The three shapes can be painted, colored, and/or glued together to be placed within the scene. In the photographed scene below, a cube is constructed from Lego pieces, a cylinder is made from rolled paper, and a star is created with toothpicks and miniature marshmallows. Miniature animals, trucks, and other items will be included in the scene for an authentic, creative project.

In the photographed scene below, featuring the letter L, items include Lego pieces, a lamp, and a ladder. Students will take a photograph of their scene and will

Lazy Lucy lingered lengthily with likeable lions, letting little Larry laugh.

Figure 4.2 Alphabet Miniature Scene

create one alliterative sentence, using the designated alphabet letter. For the scene below, the sentence reads, "Lazy Lucy lingered lengthily with likeable lions, letting little Larry laugh." Please see figure 4.2 for a photograph of the completed activity.

Highlighted Book with "Single Letter" Text Structure for Grades 7–12

Chris Van Allsburg's timeless book, *The Z Was Zapped* (1987), serves as a classic example of the "single letter" text structure in alphabet books. With its brilliant use of foreshadowing, the somewhat dark and grim illustrations appear first, followed by an impeccably perfect sentence describing the previous scene. English and drama teachers will love using this book as a clever model for vocabulary (precise word choice), alliteration, and foreshadowing (both in writing and with illustrations).

Instructional Activity with "Single Letter" Text Structure for Grades 7–12

This creative activity combines language arts (foreshadowing and alliteration) and fine arts. Teacher and students will discuss various adaptations of foreshadowing in literature and plays. Students will research various fonts and shapes of alphabet letters. The concept of "word clouds" will be explored by using Web sites such as www.tagxedo.com.

Materials for Foreshadowing and Alliteration Activity
Cardstock
Variety of art materials (watercolors, paints, pastels, markers, etc.)
Computers for researching various fonts and Web sites to create "word clouds"

Each student will create two pages similar to Van Allsburg's dramatic interpretation of alphabet letters with 26 acts. Each student will decide upon an alphabet letter, creating a "word cloud" illustration using selected words that foreshadow a second page that contains a descriptive writing assignment, utilizing alliteration, adjectives, and correct grammar and punctuation. These two-page projects can be sent to a partner elementary school for display in its library. Please see figure 4.3 for photographs of the completed activity.

Hidden Letters

Within the category called "hidden letters," alphabet books share the following characteristics:

1. Alphabet letters are hidden within illustrations
2. Alphabet letters are misshapen or distorted
3. Alphabet letters sometimes are presented out of alphabetical order
4. Text may be brief or may include a detailed storyline

Not all alphabet books with a "hidden letters" text structure possess all of the above defining characteristics, but each "hidden letter" alphabet book should contain at least

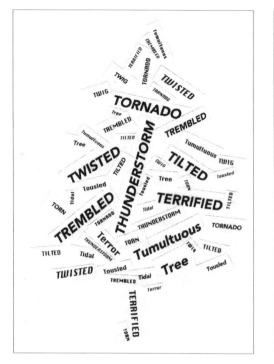

Trembling Tree

When I first heard the tumultuous winds howling outside my bedroom window, I thought I was in the middle of a terrifying dream. When I opened the blinds, the sky cracked with yellow flashes of lightning. A tall tree next to our driveway trembled and tilted against the raging thunderstorm, creating a tangled moving mass of limbs. In an instant, as if a tornado had touched down, the tree tore at its base, and the branches and twigs scattered like fragile friendships. Without thinking, I raced into the darkness and saw that the heart of the tree was still intact and strong. Over the next days we removed the tousled debris, finding comfort and solace in having strength to weather a storm.

Figure 4.3   Foreshadow and Alliteration

one of the above descriptions. The alphabet letters within "hidden letters" books are deliberately hidden or out of order to challenge students' alphabetical order schema. In some cases, these books have "letters that transform from puzzling shapes into objects and animals" (Roberts, p. 63).

Highlighted Book with "Hidden Letters" Text Structure for Pre-K–Second Grade

Within the magical world of amazing fonts lies 26 animals cleverly created by authors Sharon Werner and Sarah Forss. *Alphabeasties and Other Amazing Types* (2009) contains unique animals, each composed of the beginning letter of its name. For example, many G letters create the large, foldout giraffe's body. On the opposite page, the letter G is hidden in pictures of grapes and a girl. Both capital and lowercase letters are hidden throughout the book, making this adorable, enjoyable book an excellent representative of the "hidden letters" text structure.

Instructional Activity with "Hidden Letters" Text Structure for Pre-K–Second Grade

This basic activity combines language arts (alphabetic principle) and science (animal habitats). To reinforce the connection between a written letter (grapheme) and its phoneme, students glue an animal whose name begins with the accompanying sound of the beginning letter into the animal's natural habitat. Both capital and lowercase letters are also glued into the natural habitat, and all three items (animal, capital letter, and lowercase letter) are "hidden" behind folding windows that open into the natural habitat. Examples include a ladybug for L within a landscape of flowers and a deer for D within a forest landscape.

Materials for Letters-in-Landscapes Activity

Copies of colorful landscapes (for example, flowers, seascape, skyscape, forest)

Cutouts of animals that begin with highlighted letter

Cutouts of uppercase and lowercase highlighted letters

Glue sticks and scissors

Card stock or construction paper

Give students a piece of card stock and a background scene (natural habitat) where a certain animal might be found (e.g., ocean for a whale, sky for a bird). Students will horizontally cut the background scene into four sections and then vertically cut a flap or window in three of the four sections. Students glue all four sections onto the cardstock, like fitting together pieces of a puzzle, leaving the three vertical cuts unglued about two inches. Students will decide which animal fits within the appropriate landscape and which uppercase and lowercase letters begin the name of that animal. Students will cut out the animal and glue it into one of the vertical cuts in the background. Students will then cut out the two letters and glue them into the two remaining vertical cuts in the background. The vertical cuts can be folded to open or close, thus revealing the animal and its accompanying two letters with the beginning sound of the animal. Please see figure 4.4 for photographs of the completed activity.

Figure 4.4 Letters-in-Landscape

An excellent hands-on instructional strategy for teaching the alphabetic principle in pre-K through first-grade classrooms, student-made "hidden letter" books showcase how each lowercase letter becomes an integral part in forming an object. Each letter and object is glued onto a page of construction paper, producing a 26-page completed ABC book for students to enjoy at home while reinforcing the alphabetic principle. Please see figure 4.5 for examples of this book.

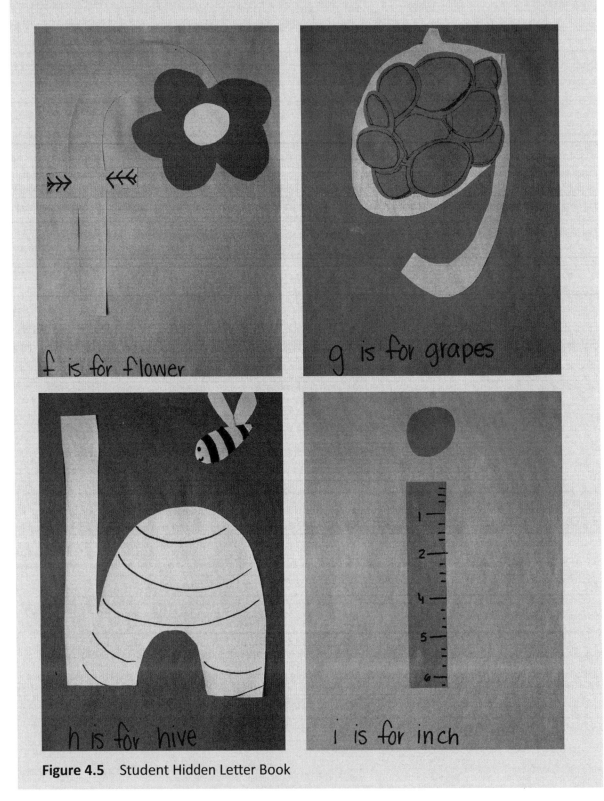

Figure 4.5   Student Hidden Letter Book

Highlighted Book with "Hidden Letters" Text Structure for Grades 3–6

In Laura Seeger's classic "hidden letter" alphabet book entitled *The Hidden Alphabet* (2003), each cleverly designed, geometric opening reveals (on the following page) a portion of a hidden letter that is beautifully composed of an accompanying object that begins with the featured letter. The use of geometric shapes enhances the visual excitement, as each page reveals an amazingly vivid capital letter.

Instructional Activity with "Hidden Letters" Text Structure for Grades 3–6

This hands-on and challenging activity combines mathematics and language arts. Teacher and students will first examine the two-page format of *The Hidden Alphabet* by Laura Seeger.

Materials for Hidden Shapes and Letter Activity
> Templates of small, medium, and large geometric shapes
> Card stock or construction paper
> Art supplies (markers, colored pencils, glue, glitter)

Students can draw or choose an alphabet letter from a box. Teacher and students brainstorm a variety of objects that begin with their designated letter and also discuss which geometric shape lends itself to the proposed object. Students will follow the teacher's modeling of gluing two pages together and cutting a geometric shape in the top page. Location

Figure 4.6   Hidden Shapes and Letters

of the geometric shape cutout in the top page is crucial, so planning and thinking of the layout can be done first as a rough draft. Students will design their second page to reveal the capital letter that is interwoven with the geometric shape. To incorporate language arts within this activity, students write a poem (couplet, limerick, or haiku) that describes their object. Please see figure 4.6 for photographs of the completed activity.

Highlighted Book with "Hidden Letters" Text Structure for Grades 7–12

In his landmark book entitled *Alphabet City* (1995), Stephen T. Johnson created beautiful watercolor illustrations of alphabet letters that are hidden in everyday objects and signs in the environment. Within the brilliant pages, letters pop from commonplace items in urban landscapes. For example, a curving brick wall forms the letter U, while the letter V is discovered as the brace of a telephone pole. Secondary school students will enjoy this amazingly unique and clever alphabet book.

Instructional Activity with "Hidden Letters" Text Structure for Grades 7–12

This hands-on activity combines technology, environmental science, and language arts. First, teacher and students will discuss various ways in which alphabet letters "appear" in natural surroundings. Second, teachers and students will explore various art books and Web sites to find examples of alphabet letters appearing in paintings, murals, and architecture. These two in-class discussions and explorations will set the stage for students finding the letters of their first or last name within the school setting (either inside or outside). For the language arts aspect, examples of acrostic poems will be modeled. To practice an acrostic poem format, students will create a three-line acrostic poem about everyday items. An acrostic poem consists of a description on each line of the vertical poem, with each line beginning with the letter that spells the featured word. For example, an acrostic poem for the word "hot" could look like the following:

Heat
Over
Town

Materials for Name-in-Nature Activity
Cell phone with camera, or digital camera
Printer with color or black ink
Yarn, ribbon, or twine
Card stock and other art supplies

Each student will locate the letters of their first or last name in the school environment, either inside or outside or both. After students have captured the letters in their natural surroundings as pictures on their cell phones, they will print these "hidden" letters in color (optional) on 8½ by 11″ paper. The letters can then be laced together with yarn or ribbon,

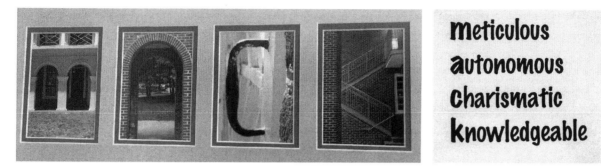

Figure 4.7   Name-in-Nature

or strung out in a vertical line. Each student will write an acrostic poem to accompany their photographs of the letters in their first or last name. Photographs and poems can be displayed in the school library or fine arts classroom. Please see figure 4.7 for photographs of the completed activity.

Conceptual Text

Within the category entitled "conceptual text," alphabet books share the following characteristics:

1. Alphabet letters are used as conduits to present concepts
2. Usually one or two letters per concept
3. Letters with accompanying concepts are presented in alphabetical order
4. Illustrations are used sparingly
5. Text may include narrative (fictional aspects) interwoven with facts

The purpose of "conceptual text" alphabet books focuses on the depiction of concepts, facts, ideas, and knowledge. All of these books present the letters in alphabetical order, and each letter highlights or signifies an important and relevant concept for that letter. Sometimes, alphabet books with a "contextual text" text structure have rhymes or jingles that begin with the letters as an anticipatory cue to the content that follows. The alphabet letters serve as conduits for presenting conceptual information—as opposed to teaching sounds and written shapes of the letters, as in the "single letter" alphabet books.

Highlighted Book with "Conceptual Text" Text Structure for Pre-K–Second Grade

George Shannon's very charming and engaging book, *Tomorrow's Alphabet* (1996), represents the "conceptual text" text structure. The letters are presented in alphabetical order but with a twist. Each letter serves as an example of cause and effect, showing what the item will become in tomorrow's world; for example, "A is for seed, Tomorrow's Apple" and "G is for bulbs, Tomorrow's Garden." Students will enjoy these clever transformations and increase their comprehension of that often difficult-to-teach concept, cause and effect.

In addition, teachers may use this book when teaching the life cycles of plants or certain animals. Thus, both language arts and science standards are featured in this book.

Instructional Activity with "Conceptual Text" Text Structure for Pre-K–Second Grade

A hands-on activity that connects science, language arts, and fine arts focuses on cause (what do plants need to grow) and effect (four parts of a living plant). By organizing pieces of brown, tan, and black construction paper to create a mosaic (as the soil), fine arts is also implemented. Teachers will review cause and effect with some examples. Teachers will discuss the necessary items for plants to grow (sun, water, soil, and seeds) and the four parts of a plant (stem, leaves, flower, and roots). Teachers will discuss the composition of various soils and reasons for choosing a particular kind of soil for growing seeds.

Materials for Plant Cause and Effect Activity
Construction paper or card stock
Green paper for stem and leaves
Paper cupcake holders (mini or regular size)
Yarn (for roots)
Yellow and orange tissue paper (for the sun)
Aluminum foil (for the raindrops)
Brown, tan, and black paper (for the soil)
Sunflower seeds
Art supplies (markers, crayons, glue, glitter)

Students will cut small pieces of brown, tan, and black paper and glue them as pieces of a mosaic along the bottom of the paper. A line will be drawn down the center of the page to separate the paper into two sections. On the left section, students will write "Causes" at the top. Sunflower seeds will be glued in the soil, and raindrops made from aluminum foil will be glued at the top. A yellow and orange tissue paper sun will also be created and glued at the top. Students will write the causes next to the items (soil, seeds, rain, and sun). On the right side of the paper, students will construct a plant, using stem and leaves (teacher-made for pre-K and kindergarten). Students will glue cupcake holders as a flower and decorate if desired. Yarn will

Figure 4.8   Plant Causes and Effects

serve as the roots. For pre-K and kindergarten, students will paste science terms (stem, leaves, flower, and roots) onto the assigned objects. Older students will label four parts of a plant and write one sentence about each plant part, including one reason why it is necessary for the life of the plant. Please see figure 4.8 for a photograph of the completed activity.

Highlighted Book with "Conceptual Text" Text Structure for Grades 3–6

As part of the dynamic *Discover America State by State* series published by Sleeping Bear Press, *O Is for Old Dominion: A Virginia Alphabet* (2005) captures the historical essence and the current attractions that lie within the state of Virginia. Author Pamela Duncan Edwards uses the alphabet letters to begin a four-line rhyme and then presents engaging facts and historical knowledge through a more complex sentence structure and a definitely elaborate vocabulary.

Knowledge of the student's state, its geographical aspects, its place within the larger American framework, and its contributions to American history takes a very large place on each state's accountability tests; TEKS (Texas Essential Knowledge and Skills) and SOL (Standards of Learning) in Virginia represent two examples of state educational accountability tests. In *O Is for Old Dominion: A Virginia Alphabet,* the letter T describes one of the five geographical regions in Virginia—"T is for Tidewater where bay and ocean both flow, along a coast that the colonists spied long ago."

Instructional Activity with "Conceptual Text" Text Structure for Grades 3–6

The following hands-on activity connects three curricular domains: geography, history, and writing (language arts). After reading *O Is for Old Dominion: A Virginia Alphabet* to supplement the classroom textbook in social studies, the teacher will reinforce the five geographical regions within Virginia through class discussion and visual aids (maps, globes, etc.). Teachers and students who reside in states other than Virginia can select their state book from the Sleeping Bear state series.

Materials for Geographical Regions Cookie Activity
    State of Virginia template or outline
    Waxed paper
    Sugar cookie dough

By viewing a Virginia state template (outline) projected upon a screen or wall, students will draw the outline of the state of Virginia onto a piece of white paper. They will next place the white paper with the Virginia outline under their waxed paper. Students will construct the state of Virginia from uncooked cookie dough on the waxed paper. Cookies are slipped from waxed paper onto cookie sheets to bake. After the state cookies have baked, students add the following:

    For Tidewater/Coastal Plain Region
        Blue icing or food sparkles for Chesapeake Bay
        White food sprinkles for sand

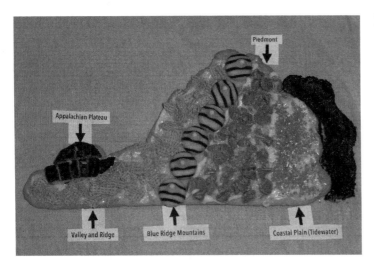

For Piedmont Region
    Chocolate chips (mini) for rolling hills
    M&M's for cities of Richmond (capital), Washington, D.C., and Charlottesville (home)
For Blue Ridge Mountains Region
    Hershey's Kisses
For Valley and Ridge Region
    Cap'n Crunch cereal
For Appalachian Plateau Region
    Rolos

Figure 4.9   Geographic Regions Cookie

Icing can be used as glue. Completed Virginia state cookies are placed onto a paper plate and given to students. Each student will write three sentences about each of the five geographical regions, using their state cookies as a guide. Please see figure 4.9 for a photograph of the completed activity.

Highlighted Book with "Conceptual Text" Text Structure for Grades 7–12

Within the secondary school curricula, the topic of careers is significant. Guidance counselors, college application tips, and personality and interest inventories provide a myriad of support and encouragement. In her dynamic book *Lights on Broadway: A Theatrical Tour from A to Z* (2009), author Harriet Ziefert depicts the challenge, the terminology, and the pizzazz of Broadway for those students considering a career in theater. From "I is for improvisation" to "V is for voice," the pages sparkle with information about the theater and acting. Bold, colorful illustrations enhance the excitement that this book creates.

Instructional Activity with "Conceptual Text" Text Structure for Grades 7–12

This hands-on, digital activity combines social studies (career options), technology, and language arts.

Materials for Digital Career Book Activity
    Pages of card stock
    Variety of art supplies for illustrations (markers, watercolors, colored pencils)

Students will discuss various careers and break into groups of similar occupational interests. For example, one group would include educators (teachers, librarians, etc.). A second group might merge under the category of scientists (doctors, lab technicians, veterinarians). Each group will decide on an inclusive career topic and research the topic via Web sites. Students will also interview a local person involved with the designated career. Each group of students will create an ABC book about their chosen career, including career terminology and illustrations. Completed books can be displayed in the school library or uploaded to the school or classroom Web site.

Figure 4.10   Digital Career Book

One example for this instructional activity centered on librarians. Below are two pages from a sample digital career book, *A Librarian's Alphabet: Excitement on Every Page*. Please see figure 4.10 for a photograph of the completed activity.

Librarians' Link

Pre-K–Second Grade

"Alphabet books are an important part of the picture book genre because concepts are communicated through both text and illustrations" (Kormanski and Stevens, p. 55). For beginning readers, concepts, such as the alphabetic principle, become the major instructional value. Alphabet books reinforce letter-shape knowledge, letter-name knowledge, letter-sound knowledge, and letter-writing ability. "Reading alphabet books is one means by which parents teach their children about the alphabet" (Bradley and Jones, p. 453).

Notable Web Sites

Listed below are instructional resources and Web sites for using alphabet books in pre-K through second grade:

www.pre-kpages.com/chicka-chicka-boom-boom-activities

From cupcake liners brimming with alphabet letters to a Play-Doh coconut tree that holds dancing letters, this Web site presents 12 adorable hands-on activities for learning the

(continued)

(*continued*)

alphabet. Based upon Eric Carle's book, and with the guidance of an early childhood consultant, this Web site will invigorate any kindergarten classroom.

www.littlegiraffes.com

This Web site is a must-see for all early childhood teachers! From Silly Sock Day to reinforce the letter S to a classroom quilt for the letter Q, this Web site is loaded with craft projects (with templates), snack ideas for alphabet learning, and lots of fun items for joyful teaching.

www.readinga-z.com/books/alphabet-book

Including a vast array of teacher ideas, this Web site devotes a section to uses of alphabet books for the early elementary classroom. Flashcards and projects for each letter are also available.

Grades 3–12

The increasing numbers of alphabet books being published for fluent readers has transformed educators' views about the uses and benefits of these ubiquitous books. "Alphabet books chosen for fluent readers should contain content that appeals to older students, as well as a more sophisticated text" (Kormanski and Stevens, p. 56).

Notable Web Sites

Listed below are instructional resources and Web sites for using alphabet books with grades 3 to 12:

www.sleepingbearpress.com/series/72-discover-america-state-by-state

Focusing on the unique characteristics of each of the fifty states, Sleeping Bear Press has published an excellent alphabet state series for upper elementary and middle schoolers. Including the nation's capital (*N Is for the Nation's Capital*) within this series, fifty-one informative books present social studies content in an enjoyable text format with realistic illustrations.

writingfix.com/Classroom-Tools-Alphabet-books

Full of creative student-made alphabet books, as well as alphabet windsocks and an alphabet math cube, this inspiring Web site will add energy and excitement to any curriculum. The emphasis on student ownership of their topic and format of homemade alphabet books rings from the pages of this colorful, dynamic teacher resource.

www.houghtonmifflinbooks.com/features/thepolarexpress/tg/zaped.shtml

Presenting exciting suggestions for teachers of middle and secondary school students, this Web site introduces Carl Van Allsburg's classic alphabet book, in which "the letters suffer alliterative mishaps and surprising situations." Educators and students will enjoy the creative uses of this book by interweaving theater arts, writing, reading strategies, and language arts.

All Grade Levels

Alphabet books enhance the curriculum in all grade levels. Versatile in their format and topic, and laden with elaborate vocabulary or presenting one word per page, alphabet books serve as engaging, excellent ways to connect students of all ages with text. "Alphabet book readings supply considerably more than information about language; they can orient children toward the ways that all book learning will be accomplished during schooling" (Smolkin and Yadin, p. 439).

Notable Web Sites

Listed below are instructional resources and Web Sites for using alphabet books with all grade levels:

jennifersommer.weebly.com

Written from a teacher's perspective, this Web site offers a thorough discussion of the importance of alphabet books, both for primary and for secondary classrooms. Several excellent alphabet books are depicted, with interesting suggestions for their instructional uses.

www.readwritethink.org (under classroom resources)

This well-known educational Web site houses many kinds of classroom resources. Ideas for using alphabet books for all grade levels are described, with a special focus on writing. Included are sample worksheets for ABC book characteristics, an ABC book checklist, and an ABC book rubric.

Works Cited

Bradley, B., and J. Jones. "Sharing Alphabet Books in Early Childhood Classrooms." *The Reading Teacher* 60 (5) (2007): 452–463. Print.

Chaney, J. H. "Alphabet Books: Resources for Learning." *The Reading Teacher* (47) (1993): 2, 96–102. Print.

Jones, M. "AB (by) C Means Alphabet Books by Children." *The Reading Teacher* 36 (1992): 646–649. Print.

Kormanski, L. M., and C. B. Stevens. "Alphabet Books Can Be Used with Fluent Readers and Writers." *Reading Horizons* (34) (1993): 1, 53–61. Print.

McGee, L., and D. Richgels. "K Is Kristen's: Learning the Alphabet from a Child's Perspective." *The Reading Teacher* (1989): 216–224. Print.

Reutzel, D. R., and R. B. Cooter Jr. *The Essentials of Teaching Children to Read: The Teacher Makes the Difference.* 3rd edition. Boston: Pearson, 2013. Print.

Roberts, P. *Alphabet: A Handbook of ABC Books and Activities for the Elementary Classroom.* Metuchen, NJ: The Scarecrow Press, 1984. Print.

Smolkin, L. B., and D. B. Yaden Jr. "O Is for Mouse: First Encounters with the Alphabet Book." *Language Arts* 69 (1992): 432–441. Print.

Chapter 5

Alphabet Books and Their Annotated Bibliographies

So please, oh PLEASE, we beg, we pray,
Go throw your TV set away,
And in its place you can install,
A lovely bookshelf on the wall.
Roald Dahl, *Charlie and the Chocolate Factory*

The list below of over 300 alphabet books, deemed appropriate for public and private school settings, was selected for instructional value, accessibility, and artistic creativity. Special attention was given to including alphabet books that appeal to all grade levels and present a variety of topics.

List of Alphabet Books, Arranged by Topic

Animals	Health and Activity	Nature
Arts	History	Objects
Careers	Holidays	Poetry/Short Story
Children	Mathematics	Science
Classic Characters	Mixed-Up Alphabet	Transportation
Fantasy	Multicultural	Urban

Animals

Title *ABC Animal Jamboree*
Author Giles Andreae
Illustrator David Wojtowycz
Publishing Company/Date Tiger Tales/2010

ISBN# 978-1589250925

Summary Showcasing a wide range of animals that swim, jump, and fly, this bold and cheerful ABC book offers four to five lines of catchy rhymes that highlight, from the animal's perspective, its unique behavior or characteristic. From mooching in the mud to slithering on icebergs, each letter is clearly presented in both uppercase and lowercase and is boxed in a contrasting color.

Grades Pre-K–2

Content Area Language Arts

Instructional Value Rhyme and rhythm

Text Structure Single letter (expanded)

Title *K Is for Kissing a Cool Kangaroo*

Author Giles Andreae

Illustrator Guy Parker-Rees

Publishing Company/Date Orchard Books/2003

ISBN# 978-0439531269

Summary Each cartoon scene is composed of a variety of animals and objects whose names begin with the featured letter. The simple narrative sentence "A is for apple that grows on a tree" is expanded in the illustration to include an aardvark balancing on an ant-eater, each trying to reach the apple, while an antelope and an armadillo look on. The humorous and detailed illustrations capture the playful interaction among the animals. Capital and lowercase letters are in a bold and contrasting color in an upper corner. A complete listing of objects is in the back of the book.

Grades Pre-K–2

Content Area Language Arts

Instructional Value Alphabetic principle; phonemic awareness

Text Structure Single letter (expanded)

Title *Name That Dog! Puppy Poems from A to Z*

Author Peggy Archer

Illustrator Stephanie Buscema

Publishing Company/Date Dial Books/2010

ISBN# 978-0803733220

Summary Each capital letter begins dog's name that perfectly fits that dog's personality or unique characteristic. For example, Bandit steals socks, and Daisy likes to nap in the flowers. The poems vary in length and make use of clever language and witty phrasing. "Xerox/ From the tops of his ears/to the tip of his tail/and everything else in between—/He couldn't have looked/any more like his dad/If he'd come from a copy machine!" The illustrations have a retro feel and show the dogs in action, emphasizing the shaggy fur, floppy ears, or speckled coat characteristic of their breed. The breed's name is included in a corner.

Grades Pre-K–2

Content Area Language Arts

Instructional Value Rhyme and rhythm
Text Structure Single letter (expanded)

Title *Naughty Little Monkeys*
Author Jim Aylesworth
Illustrator Henry Cole
Publishing Company/Date Dutton Children's Books/2003
ISBN# 978-0525469407
Summary Twenty-six mischievous monkeys won't go to sleep while their parents are out for the evening; instead, they swing on the drapes, get gum on the chair, spill syrup over the counters, slide down the banister, and splash water out of the tub. Each of the four-lined rhymed verses associated with a letter of the alphabet describes their exuberant actions, and the vibrant and expressive illustrations highlight their comedic antics. The letters are presented in capital form within a colorful frame. The story ends with the parents taking these monkey siblings to the zoo for a day of fun.
Grades Pre-K–2
Content Area Language Arts
Instructional Value Rhyme and rhythm
Text Structure Single letter (expanded)

Title *The A to Z Beastly Jamboree*
Author/Illustrator Robert Bender
Publishing Company/Date Lodestar Books/1996
ISBN# 978-0525675204
Summary With jewel-toned, spray-paint-styled illustrations, each letter appears as a unique character within the scene. The "A" bobs in the ocean tethered to the sea bottom by an anchor while ants climb about, making sure all is secure. The phrase "Ants anchor Aa" is written below. Each letter is presented in capital and lowercase form in a contrasting color. There is a frame consisting of 26 animals around each page, initially composed of a line of 26 ants for the letter A; with each successive letter, a new animal is introduced, so that for the letter Z, where "Zebras zipper Zz," all 26 tiny animals frame the scene.
Grades Pre-K–2
Content Area Language Arts
Instructional Value Alliteration
Text Structure Single letter

Title *ABC ZooBorns!*
Author Andrew Bleiman and Chris Eastland
Photographer Various
Publishing Company/Date Beach Lane Books/2012
ISBN# 978-1442443716

Summary Cute, close-up photographs of tiny newborn animals are the subjects for the letters of the alphabet. From the baby anteater with its extra-long tongue, to the baby hippopotamus playing in the water, to the yawning sloth, each animal is accompanied with a two- or three-sentence text that describes the scene. The letters of the alphabet are in capital form and appear in a contrasting color. An outline of the animal nestles next to the letter. A listing of the animals in the back of the book offers species, home, and conservation status as well as a paragraph description of habitat, food, or unique characteristics.
Grades Pre-K–2
Content Area Science
Instructional Value Life science
Text Structure Single letter (expanded)

Title *A Is for Musk Ox*
Author Erin Cabatingan
Illustrator Matthew Myers
Publishing Company/Date Roaring Book Press/2012
ISBN# 978-1596436763
Summary The banter between a cantankerous, self-centered musk ox and an uptight zebra offers much hilarious dialogue. The collage element of plastering "musk ox" over all previous word associations for each letter of the alphabet helps build the cheeky and playful storyline. It is the narrative that makes the association with the musk ox clear. "A is for musk ox," because, among other things, "a musk ox is awesome." The painted illustrations are colorful, and the dialogue is presented in quick bursts scattered about the page. For the letter C, a "cool" musk ox wearing sunglasses is shown relaxing on a recliner in an icy room. The bold letters are shown in both capital and lowercase.
Grades 3–6
Content Area Language Arts
Instructional Value Descriptive writing
Text Structure Single letter (expanded)

Title *D Is for Dinosaur: A Prehistoric Alphabet*
Author Todd Chapman and Lita Judge
Illustrator Lita Judge
Publishing Company/Date Sleeping Bear Press/2007
ISBN# 978-1585362424
Summary Ideal for the budding paleontologist, this book is full of facts and explores current discoveries, even those made by children themselves. Each letter is presented in both uppercase and lowercase and is the beginning letter for a general term, like "B is for Bonebed" or "U is for Unknown." A side panel for each letter offers more detailed information, while the text set inside the engaging illustration offers a simpler, rhyming verse for the younger reader.

Grades 3–6
Content Area Language Arts and Science
Instructional Value Rhyme and rhythm; earth science
Text Structure Conceptual text

Title *Click, Clack, Quackity-Quack*
Author Doreen Cronin
Illustrator Betsy Lewin
Publishing Company/Date Atheneum Books for Young Readers/2005
ISBN# 978-0689877155
Summary Each lowercase letter is presented and then used in a short (often two-word) alliterative phrase that tells the delightful story of a myriad of barnyard animals gathering for a duck-led excursion. Hints of their ultimate destination are scattered throughout the book, but the answer—a picnic spot—is only fully revealed at the end, allowing for a sense of suspense. The last page shows all of the animals asleep, making this story ideal for bedtime reading. The loosely outlined watercolor illustrations show movement and cheery camaraderie among these familiar animals.
Grades Pre-K–2
Content Area Language Arts
Instructional Value Alliteration
Text Structure Single letter

Title *All the Awake Animals Are Almost Asleep*
Author Crescent Dragonwagon
Illustrator David McPhail
Publishing Company/Date Little, Brown and Company/2012
ISBN# 978-0316070454
Summary In this charming text, each letter of the alphabet is presented in large, sweeping, cursive form and again within a lyrical and alliterative narrative that describes how each animal prepares for sleep. The name of the animal is capitalized within the text; for example, "Cat's curled up on a crimson couch cushion" and "Each evening, Elephant eases her elegant ears and edges into sleep." The watercolor-and-ink illustrations are soft and gentle enough to encourage a young mind to relax and dream.
Grades Pre-K–2
Content Area Language Arts and Science
Instructional Value Alliteration; vocabulary; life science
Text Structure Single letter (expanded)

Title *Bang! Boom! Roar! A Busy Crew of Dinosaurs*
Author Nate Evans and Stephanie Gwyn Brown
Illustrator Christopher Santoro
Publishing Company/Date HarperCollins Children's Books/2012

ISBN# 978-0060879600

Summary Dinosaurs and trucks is a winning combination. Each letter begins the zippy, four-lined rhyme that tells the story of a collection of cartoon dinosaurs that form a construction crew. The outcome of their busy labors is not known until the end, when all enjoy the water park wonderland. Hidden letters are scattered throughout the book, and the photographic collage elements and graphic illustrations give an urban, gritty, yet playful vibe. This book is chock-full of details, and even the youngest reader will find visual enjoyment.

Grades Pre-K–2

Content Area Language Arts

Instructional Value Alliteration; rhyme and rhythm; vocabulary

Text Structure Hidden letter

Title *My Little Sister Hugged an Ape*

Author Bill Grossman

Illustrator Kevin Hawkes

Publishing Company/Date Alfred A. Knopf/2004

ISBN# 978-0517800171

Summary This little sister isn't afraid of any animal she sees; in fact, all she wants to do is hug them. The disastrous results are hilarious, and the four-line rhyme for each letter of the alphabet describes each slimy, icky, and disgusting interaction. Every letter is connected to a type of animal whose name appears in all capital letters within the poem. Animals range from ape to goat, jackal, newt, octopus, rat, and yak. The illustrations play up the exuberance of the young girl with her wide grin and playful nature and the wide-eyed shock of each animal. The only one left to hug at the end of the book is her brother.

Grades Pre-K–2

Content Area Language Arts

Instructional Value Rhyme and rhythm

Text Structure Single letter (expanded)

Title *African Animal Alphabet*

Photographer Beverly Joubert and Dereck Joubert

Publishing Company/Date National Geographic Children's Books/2011

ISBN# 978-1426307829

Summary With signature National Geographic quality, 26 exceptional close-up photographs of Africa's most amazing animals are showcased. Each animal is described with two or three sentences, and the letter featured is in uppercase form and again capitalized at the beginning of the animal name. A "Did you know?" text box appears in an upper corner with an interesting additional fact. A thumbnail photo spread of all the animals with home, size, food, sounds, and babies offers a chance to compare the animals with each other. A one-page glossary offers simple definitions for words such as "desert," "elongated," "rain forest" and "venom." Additional reference books and Web sites for further exploration are also given.

Grades 3–6
Content Area Science
Instructional Value Life science
Text Structure Conceptual text

Title *Boo ABC: A to Z with the World's Cutest Dog*
Author J. H. Lee
Photographer Gretchen Le Maistre
Publishing Company/Date Chronicle Books/2013
ISBN# 978-1452109190
Summary Arguably the world's cutest dog is photographed throughout its fun-filled day. From A, "Awake" ("Rise and shine! Time to wake up and start the day!") through "Car," "Eat," "Run," and "Yawn," this fluffy, bright-eyed dog is adorable and looks eager to keep on playing. Each letter is presented in capital form and paired with one word. A short sentence shares a friendly detail, and the photographs are crisp and colorful.
Grades Pre-K–2
Content Area Language Arts
Instructional Value Alphabetic principle
Text Structure Single letter (expanded)

Title *Animal Antics: A to Z*
Author/ Illustrator Anita Lobel
Publishing Company/Date Greenwillow Books/2005
ISBN# 978-0060518141
Summary In this entertaining circus-themed book, a pair of identical animals for every letter of the alphabet is presented with an associated adjective, from the more familiar animals like Adoring Alligators and Romping Rabbits to the less common, such as Impish Ibexes and Nice Nylas. A consistent illustrative frame is used that includes a drawn curtain and a tightrope above, with a pair of gymnasts forming the featured letter with their bodies. The illustrations are full of color, texture, and pattern. Some animals even sport hats and bow ties. A page in the back shares facts about each of the animals, including where they live and what they can do.
Grades Pre-K–2
Content Area Language Arts
Instructional Value Alliteration; phonemic awareness
Text Structure Hidden letter

Title *Playful Pigs from A to Z*
Author/Illustrator Anita Lobel

Publishing Company/Date Knopf Books for Young Readers/2015

ISBN# 978-0553508338

Summary Each pig is illustrated standing on a gently rolling field next to a giant, colorful capital letter that also begins the pig's name and depicted action. Brief alliterative sentences include "Amanda Pig admired an A," "Billy Pig balanced on a B," and "Clara Pig cleaned a C." An additional object—often a fruit, vegetable or flower—also beginning with the featured letter, is in a lower corner. At the end of this fun-filled day, all of the pigs return to their pen for the night. On each page, the entire alphabet in capital letters forms an upper border and the lowercase letters form the lower border. The watercolor illustrations are folksy and full of charming details, like a beret, flowered shirt, and overalls for "Denzel Pig drew a D."

Grades Pre-K–2

Content Area Language Arts

Instructional Value Alliteration; alphabetic principle

Text Structure Single letter (expanded)

Title *Zoopa: An Animal Alphabet*

Author/Illustrator Gianna Marino

Publishing Company/Date Chronicle Books/2005

ISBN# 978-0811847896

Summary A large bowl of tomato soup sits on a yellow placemat, and with each spread, two or three animals are introduced to the scene with their associated capital letter. Only the illustrated animal and letter appear, and as subsequent animals enter, the scene becomes more crowded; some of the animals interact with one another or swim in the soup. Most animals are easily recognizable, but two spreads in the back of the book show all of the animals labeled with their names, which will help identify more unusual animals, like quail or xenops.

Grades Pre-K–2

Content Area Language Arts

Instructional Value Phonemic awareness

Text Structure Single letter

Title *Gone Wild: An Endangered Animal Alphabet*

Author/Illustrator David McLimans

Publishing Company/Date Walker & Company/2006

ISBN# 978-0802795649

Summary Graphic black-and-white illustrations depict a range of endangered animals, from the Chinese alligator to Grey's zebra. Using individual capital letters as a base, feathers, scales, fur, teeth, and claws sprout to create the stylized animal. A smaller illustration in red shows the complete animal form. The overall design is striking, with great visual interest. The capital and lowercase letter are presented in red in an upper corner and again in red within the name of the animal. Class, habitat, range, threats, and status are provided in a text box. An appendix details unique traits of these animals. Web sites and books for further understanding are also presented. *Caldecott Honor Book*

Grades 3–6

Content Area Fine Arts and Science

Instructional Value Observation and perceptions; life science

Text Structure Hidden letter

Title *My Sound Parade*

Author Jane Belk Moncure

Illustrator Colin King

Publishing Company/Date The Child's World/2001

ISBN# 978-1567667660

Summary Each lowercase letter is attached to the shirt or hat of a young child participating in the alphabetic parade. The narrative announces each letter's arrival: "Here comes little b with a baby baboon and a bear on a bicycle with a balloon." The alliterative choices include many familiar animals and objects. Carefully shaded illustrations, with fine black outlines, sweetly depict the smiling animals and a proud and diverse parade of children. A collection of all of the animals appears at the end of the book with an invitation for readers to join in the fun.

Grades Pre-K–2

Content Area Language Arts

Instructional Value Alliteration; phonemic awareness

Text Structure Single letter (expanded)

Title *Apple Pie ABC*

Author/Illustrator Alison Murray

Publishing Company/Date Hyperion Books/2011

ISBN# 978-1423136941

Summary In this charming retelling of a traditional poem, a playful puppy wants to eat a freshly baked apple pie, and throughout the entire alphabet, he longs for it and tries to get a taste. The vivid vintage textile illustrations create the simple connection between the dog and the pie he so eagerly wants to eat. Each capital letter begins a word or phrase associated with the pie, such as "Apple Pie," "Bake it," "Cool it," and "Dish it out." The dog's young pigtailed owner is a lovely additional character in this story.

Grades Pre-K–2

Content Area Language Arts

Instructional Value Vocabulary

Text Structure Single letter

Title *The Beetle Alphabet Book*

Author Jerry Pallotta

Illustrator David Biedrzycki

Publishing Company/Date Charlesbridge/2004

ISBN# 978-1570915512

Summary This book is a fascinating look at the diverse species of beetles. Each page highlights a beetle whose name begins with one of the letters of the alphabet. A few non-beetles are slipped in to test readers, as all things that crawl aren't necessarily beetles. The bold uppercase and lowercase letters often have a black- or white-colored beetle within the design of the letter. The illustrations are precise and show the beetle in action. The color, proportion, and texture of the beetles are precise. An interesting fact is mentioned in the text, and some humor is included, like if the two elephant stag beetles don't stop fighting, they might be sent to the principal's office. There are many other alphabet books created by Jerry Pallotta covering a wide range of topics.

Grades Pre-K–2

Content Area Science

Instructional Value Life science

Text Structure Conceptual text

Title *A Paddling of Ducks: Animals in Groups from A to Z*

Author Marjorie Blain Parker

Illustrator Joseph Kelly

Publishing Company/Date Kids Can Press/2010

ISBN# 978-1553376828

Summary In this richly detailed and captivating book, each animal group is described using a collective noun, with the name of the animal highlighted and the letter presented in uppercase and lowercase in the bottom left corner. The playful animals are dressed and doing what people do: the aardvark is working on his laptop, donut and coffee by his side; the moles wear construction hats and dig tunnels using tiny construction equipment; a school of X-ray fish wear graduation caps and swim in formation. The ducks make an appearance in every scene.

Grades Pre-K–2

Content Area Science

Instructional Value Life science

Text Structure Single letter (expanded)

Title *Alligator in an Anorak*

Author/Illustrator Daron Parton

Publishing Company/Date Random House/2014

ISBN# 978-0857983091

Summary In this offbeat and playful book, an animal and an object beginning with the same letter are paired, doing unusual things at an unusual scale. The elephant is perched in an eggcup, the hippo flies in a helicopter, the newt wears a necktie, and the urchin is wearing his undies. The letter of the alphabet that begins the name of the animal and the animal's activity or object is capitalized and in a contrasting color. Presented on a white background, the colorful and quirky illustrations include collage elements that offer texture and give the whole book a whimsical quality.

Grades Pre-K–2

Content Area Language Arts

Instructional Value Phonemic awareness

Text Structure Single letter

Title *A Swim through the Sea*

Author/Illustrator Kristin Joy Pratt

Publishing Company/Date Dawn Publications/1994

ISBN# 978-1883220044

Summary Seamore the seahorse invites readers to join him as he explores the fascinating undersea world. On each page an alliterative phrase like "He'd admire an amiable Angelfish in appealing apparel" is followed by a comprehensive paragraph that details the habits and habitat of the sea animal. A frame of other sea animals starting with the same letter surrounds the colorful watercolors. A capital letter is clearly presented in a corner of the illustration. In the introduction, this 16-year-old author and artist encourages young people to preserve the delicate balance of the oceans.

Grades 7–12

Content Area Language Arts and Science

Instructional Value Alliteration; earth science; life science

Text Structure Conceptual text

Title *Tickets to Ride: An Alphabetic Amusement*

Author/Illustrator Mark Rogalski

Publishing Company/Date Running Press Kids/2006

ISBN# 978-0762427826

Summary On the left page, readers are presented a uniquely designed entrance ticket with an alluring rhyme. The ticket invites the reader to enter the ride presented on the right. From the alligator airplane to the zebra zeppelin, each imaginative illustration of computer graphics is suggestive of animation. The individual letters of the alphabet are not highlighted themselves, but instead they serve as an organizational device. Younger children will be fascinated with the illustrations; older children will find the rhyming text intriguing and mysterious. Embedded in each picture is a number from 1 to 26. Readers can also search for the duck. In the back, a full-page spread shows the entire amusement park.

Grades Pre-K–2

Content Area Language Arts

Instructional Value Descriptive writing

Text Structure Single letter (expanded)

Title *Into the A, B, Sea*
Author Deborah Lee Rose
Illustrator Steve Jenkins
Publishing Company/Date Scholastic Press/2000
ISBN# 978-0439096966
Summary Taking a deep dive into the ocean, this grouping of 26 ocean animals and plants swims and sways in the superb paper collage illustrations. The texture, coloring, and movement is artfully captured, beginning with "Anemones sting and Barnacles cling where Crabs crawl in and Dolphins spin, where Eels explore and Flying fish soar, where Gray whales peep and Humpbacks leap." Some of the animals are presented on an entire spread, rather than just a page, further emphasizing their strength and beauty. The rhyming text is succinct and lyrical. A capital letter appears as the beginning of the featured word. A glossary at the end gives additional information.
Grades Pre-K–2
Content Area Language Arts and Science
Instructional Value Rhyme and rhythm; life science
Text Structure Single letter (expanded)

Title *Beautiful Birds*
Author Jean Roussen
Illustrator Emmanuelle Walker
Publishing Company/Date Flying Eye Books/2015
ISBN# 978-1909263291
Summary Beautifully composed graphic designs feature birds of 26 varieties, each captivatingly presented with a bold palette. A brief poetic text ("E is for egret: its yellow eyes that pierce/and E is for eagle, majestic but fierce") presents the featured letter, capitalized within the text. Each page is devoted to a type of bird, and the view may be close up or distant but always is a visual delight.
Grades Pre-K–2
Content Area Fine Arts
Instructional Value Graphic arts
Text Structure Single letter (expanded)

Title *The ABC Animal Orchestra*
Author/Illustrator Donald Saaf
Publishing Company/Date Henry Holt and Company/2015
ISBN# 978-0805090727
Summary This book associates each of the letters of the alphabet with an animal and a musical instrument from around the world. The text is charming and alliterative, and the letters are presented in bold capital form. Colorful illustrations incorporate collage elements that have a folk art feel. Animals wear clothes and dance about, joyfully creating their music.

Grades Pre-K–2

Content Area Language Arts

Instructional Value Alphabetic principle; vocabulary

Text Structure Single letter (expanded)

Title *Airdale to Zuchon: Dogs from A to Z*

Author Mary Elizabeth Salzmann

Photographer Various

Publishing Company/Date ABDO Publishing Company/2009

ISBN# 978-1604534917

Summary This alphabetical tour of dogs highlights the unique and identifying characteristics of 26 breeds with a crisp photograph for each as well as the breed's average height and weight. Some of the breeds included are bloodhound, chihuahua, mastiff and Rhodesian ridgeback. A one- or two-sentence description often repeats the name of the breed, which appears in a contrasting color. The featured letter is presented in capital and lowercase in an upper corner. A "Guess what?" bubble offers an interesting fact or a helpful pronunciation guide.

Grades Pre-K–2

Content Area Language Arts and Science

Instructional Value Vocabulary; life science

Text Structure Conceptual Text

Title *We're All in the Same Boat*

Author Zachary R. Shapiro

Illustrator Jack E. Davis

Publishing Company/Date G. P. Putnam's Sons/2009

ISBN# 978-0399243936

Summary Using the framework of the story of Noah's ark, 26 pairs of animals become restless after a few months at sea. "The ants were antsy. The bees were bored. The camels were complaining." When they all look to blame Noah, Noah replies, "We're all in the same boat!" Then another tour of the alphabet ensues, but this time with good humor and friendliness: "The ants apologized and the bees behaved." The letters appear in lowercase at the beginning of the name of the associated animal and verb. The pen and watercolor illustrations are both charming and hilarious. The animals are expressive and often wear flowered hats, eyeglasses, and pearls, and the backdrop of a luxury cruise liner, complete with banners, squash rackets, and lounge chairs, provides fun details.

Grades Pre-K–2

Content Area Language Arts

Instructional Value Alliteration

Text Structure Single letter (expanded)

Title *Shiver Me Letters: A Pirate ABC*
Author June Sobel
Illustrator Henry Cole
Publishing Company/Date HMH Books for Young Readers/2009
ISBN# 978-0152066796
Summary A ragtag crew of animals, including an alligator captain, sets sail in this pirate adventure. Their goal is to capture all of the letters of the alphabet. The rhyming text describes each discovery, and the letters are presented in boldface within the text. Further, each letter is hidden in the cartoon illustration; it may be floating in the water, in a treasure chest, or on the back of a turtle. The humorous text includes the animals interacting with the letters and the captain roaring "R!"
Grades Pre-K–2
Content Area Language arts
Instructional Value Rhyme and rhythm
Text Structure Hidden letters

Title *The Dog on the Bed: A Canine Alphabet*
Author Richard Teleky
Publishing Company/Date Fitzhenry & Whiteside/2011
ISBN# 978-1554552191
Summary One short essay or more is presented for each letter of the alphabet, with wide-ranging topics that will appeal to any dog lover. Topics include anthropomorphism, breeds, communication, noses, and therapy, and they cover personal reflections, interesting dog facts, and thoughtful insights. The letters of the alphabet appear in capital form at the beginning of the word for the chapter. Here the alphabet is a device to give linkage and structure to the essays. The chapters can be read in any order, and the overall feel is entertaining and heartwarming.
Grades 7–12
Content Area Language Arts
Instructional Value Descriptive writing; vocabulary
Text Structure Conceptual text

Title *Caveman, A B.C. Story*
Author/Illustrator Janee Trasler
Publishing Company/Date Sterling Children's Books/2011
ISBN# 978-1402771194
Summary The clever title hints at the zany tale of a caveman and a squirrel on the hunt for the ever-elusive acorn. Each letter in the alphabet begins a word (like "Eat," "Leave," and "Run") that narrates a simple but active storyline. The capital letter is presented in a different color. In the end, all are happily exhausted, making this a bedtime read as well.
Grades Pre-K–2

Content Area Language Arts
Instructional Value Alphabetic principle
Text Structure Single letter

Title *Alphabeasties and Other Amazing Animal Types*
Author/Illustrator Sharon Werner and Sarah Foss
Publishing Company/Date Blue Apple Books/2009
ISBN# 978-1934706787
Summary The letters themselves, presented in interesting fonts, become the framework for each animal in this alphabet tour. Multiple repetitions of the letter A form the body of an alligator, with a lowercase A indicating an eye and an upside-down capital A referencing a claw. The ends of the letter S curl to form the wooly coat of the sheep. Additional words form a band along the bottom edge, including comments on type styles. Several pages include a flap that opens to offer a different view; the page for the letter G has two flaps to open, revealing a tall giraffe behind the lush vegetation.
Grades Pre-K–2
Content Area Fine Arts and Language Arts
Instructional Value Graphic design; phonemic awareness
Text Structure Single letter (expanded)

Title *Alphasaurs and Other Prehistoric Types*
Author/Illustrator Sharon Werner and Sarah Forss
Publishing Company/Date Blue Apple Books/2012
ISBN# 978-1609051938
Summary Illustrations of every imaginable dinosaur are created using many individual letters of the alphabet. The iguanodon is composed of hundreds of tiny capital and lowercase I's. The font style is selected to match the animal's personality. Have you heard of the euoplocephalus, the iguanodon, or the xenoposeidon? Well, they are in here! Facts from the general to the obscure are scattered along the bottom of the page along with a pronunciation guide. Artful folding flaps allow the reader to unearth even more treasures.
Grades 3–6
Content Area Science
Instructional Value Earth science
Text Structure Conceptual text

Title *A Zeal of Zebras: An Alphabet of Collective Nouns*
Author/Illustrator Woop Studios
Publishing Company/Date Chronicle Books/2011
ISBN# 978-1452104928
Summary Strong graphics with textured collage elements offer a sophisticated design that showcases the collective nouns for 26 animal groups. These include an "Aurora of Polar

Bears," a "Bale of Turtles," a "Caravan of Camels," and a "Down of Rabbits." Even the X, a tricky letter to handle, is an "Exaltation of Larks." The capital letter appears in the corner of the illustration, in a stylized font next to the collective noun. The accompanying narrative of two short paragraphs is a tribute to what makes these animals so majestic and alluring.

Grades 3–6
Content Area Fine Arts
Instructional Value Descriptive writing; graphic design
Text Structure Single letter (expanded)

Title *Creature ABC*
Author/Photographer Andrew Zuckerman
Publishing Company/Date Chronicle Books LLC/2009
ISBN# 978-0811869782
Summary Each featured animal, from alligator to zebra, is shown in two captivating photographs against a white background. The first is a close-up of the animal paired with the letter in both capital and lowercase. The second shows most, if not all, of the entire animal in a different pose, with the name of the animal beside it. Animal lovers will be fascinated by the extraordinary detail; every hair, scale, and feather is crisp and clear. A four-page glossary gives a thumbnail picture of each animal, its corresponding letter, and an interesting fact or two to encourage readers to explore further.

Grades Pre-K–2
Content Area Science
Instructional Value Life science
Text Structure Single letter

Arts

Title *Roy Lichtenstein's ABC*
Author Bob Adelman
Illustrator Roy Lichtenstein
Publishing Company/Date Bulfinch Press Book/1999
ISBN# 978-0821225912
Summary Every two-page spread pairs the capital letter and associated word(s) on the left page with a hard-edged, precise illustration on the right page. The illustrations are taken from a print, drawing or painting by pop artist Roy Lichtenstein, whose own language of dots and lines is often associated with comic book art. The capital letter is in a bold, attention-grabbing, graphic style. A is associated with art; B is associated with barn, black, and blue; C is associated with cup, coffee, and curves.

Grades Pre-K–2
Content Area Fine Arts

Instructional Value Graphic design; observation and perception

Text Structure Single letter

Title *Anno's Alphabet: An Adventure in Imagination*

Author/ Illustrator Mitsumasa Anno

Publishing Company/Date HarperCollins /1975

ISBN# 978-0690005417

Summary In this finely illustrated book, each capital letter on the left page is drawn as if formed by bending or joining pieces of wood. On closer inspection, the letters play an Escher-like trick on the eyes. The facing page depicts an object whose name begins with that letter, often including a wooden element, like a bicycle with a wooden wheel, or an umbrella with a wooden handle. A detailed, black-and-white, vegetal frame surrounds the entire spread; hidden amid these branches are additional animals or flowers whose names start with the letter featured. A listing of all of the items found on each page is provided in the back of the book.

Grades All ages

Content Area Fine Arts

Instructional Value Observation and perception

Text Structure Hidden letter

Title *ABC3D*

Author/Illustrator Marion Bataille

Publishing Company/Date Roaring Book Press/2008

ISBN# 978-1596434257

Summary This is an innovative three-dimensional pop-up book that cleverly plays on the transitioning of one letter to the next. The bottom piece of the E slips away to form the F. The O and P both add a short diagonal piece, transforming them into Q and R. Each letter is presented in capital form, and the reduced palette of red, black, and white gives focus to the fine design and sculptural forms of the letters.

Grades All ages

Content Area Fine Arts

Instructional Value Observation and perception

Text Structure Hidden letter

Title *The Turn-Around, Upside-Down Alphabet Book*

Author/Illustrator Lisa Campbell Ernst

Publishing Company/Date Simon & Schuster Books for Young Readers/2004

ISBN# 978-0689856853

Summary In this truly interactive book, each page displays a colorful capital letter set inside a contrastingly colored square. The text is written along all four sides of the square, requiring the reader to rotate the book in order to read the text. Each rotation then describes how the letter appears from that angle. The interplay between the positive and negative spaces of the letter within the square creates the opportunity to see something new and offers the reader a challenge to see this too. The K, for example, becomes a picnic table or a Martian's antennae when viewed from each side and a mama duck and duckling when viewed upside down.

Grades Pre-K–2

Content Area Fine Arts

Instructional Value Observation and perception

Text Structure Hidden letter

Title *Alphabet Under Construction*

Author/Illustrator Denise Fleming

Publishing Company/Date Henry Holt and Company/2002

ISBN# 978-080506848

Summary An industrious, buck-toothed mouse creates each letter of the alphabet using a different art technique. "Mouse airbrushes the A, buttons the B, carves the C, dyes the D." In each engaging scene, the giant capital letter is being constructed by the mouse, and the letter appears again in capital form within the text. The rainbow-colored, richly saturated illustrations show the creative zeal of the mouse and the tools and basic process needed for each technique. A calendar at the end shows the mouse's work schedule, where some side notes on project planning are also listed (e.g., "Pick up new spatula," "Coffee with Peter," and "Call Mom").

Grades Pre-K–2

Content Area Language Arts

Instructional Value Alphabetic principle

Text Structure Single letter

Title *A Is for Art: An Abstract Alphabet*

Author/Illustrator Stephen T. Johnson

Publishing Company/Date Simon & Schuster Books for Young Readers/2008

ISBN# 978-0689863011

Summary This book is like a stroll through a contemporary art museum. The author created and then photographed 26 abstract works of art based on words that start with each letter of the alphabet. Some are large-scale sculptures, and others are paintings. A complex and intriguing alliterative sentence describes the work of art. The letters are presented in both capital and lowercase and are also hidden within the artwork. An index offers thumb-sized reproductions of each piece, revealing the locations of the hidden letters.

Grades 3–6 and 7–12

Content Area Fine Arts and Language Arts

Instructional Value Observation and perception; alliteration; vocabulary

Text Structure Hidden letter

Title *Alphabet City*
Author/Illustrator Stephen T. Johnson
Publishing Company/Date Viking/1995
ISBN# 978-0670856312

Summary In these superb, photorealistic watercolors and pastels, each capital letter is presented on a single page. What is commonplace becomes an opportunity for discovery. The side of an old sawhorse becomes the A, and a wrought-iron banister becomes the J. No words or people appear, just the pure forms, sometimes close up, and sometimes from a bird's-eye view. This book invites students to explore the everyday in the city and to discover and delight in the alphabet around them.
Caldecott Honor Book
Grades All ages
Content Area Fine Arts
Instructional Value Observation and perception
Text Structure Hidden letter

Title *Alphabet School*
Author/Illustrator Stephen T. Johnson
Publishing Company/Date Simon & Schuster Books for Young Readers/2015
ISBN# 978-14169-25217

Summary In this wordless look through classrooms, the library, and the playground, each capital letter of the alphabet can be found. The large, yellow stepladder in the library, as seen from the side, creates the letter A. The shadows of the school bus's side mirror create a darkened B. The golden curve of the globe stand near a classroom windowsill creates the letter C. The illustrations are presented as if they were faded photographs that have been stippled with age, giving a quiet timelessness to the images. Here the visual form of the letters is explored within a new context, encouraging readers to be visually aware to the possibilities of discovery around them.
Grades Pre-K–2
Content Area Fine Arts
Instructional Value Observation and perception
Text Structure Hidden letter

Title *Ah-Ha to Zig-Zag: 31 Objects from Cooper Hewitt, Smithsonian Design Museum*
Author/ Illustrator Maira Kalman
Publishing Company/Date Skira Rizzoli/2014
ISBN# 978-0847843770

Summary Treasures from the Cooper Hewitt museum are celebrated in this delightfully designed book featuring everyday objects from the 5th century to the 20th. The objects are linked together by fanciful, humorous text describing their purpose in whimsical detail. The illustrations are bold and representative. A spread in the back of the book shows thumbnail photos of the actual objects that inspired the book, along with identifying information. There is also an invitation for the reader to write to the museum and to consider what objects they might want to put in their own museum collection.

Grades 3–6 and 7–12

Content Area Fine Arts and Language Arts

Instructional Value Observation and perception; descriptive writing

Text Structure Single letter (expanded)

Title *M Is for Music*

Author Kathleen Krull

Illustrator Stacy Innerst

Publishing Company/Date Harcourt, Inc./2003

ISBN# 978-0152014384

Summary This musical alphabet runs the scales from favorite tunes and unusual instruments to famous musicians and musical terms. The alphabet is presented in uppercase and lowercase, and on each page several musical words beginning with that letter are presented, both in a sentence and scattered about the page. Some words (like "dancing," "guitar," and "radio") may be more familiar, but the majority of the words are less common for those new to music, such as "Hildegard of Bingen," "klezmer," "ukulele," "yodeling," and "zydeco." A glossary explains one of the target words for each letter and repeats the letter in both uppercase and lowercase form. The painted illustrations are soft-edged, muted, and artfully composed.

Grades Pre-K–2

Content Area Fine Arts and Language Arts

Instructional Value Observation and perception; alphabetic principle; vocabulary

Text Structure Single letter (expanded)

Title *If Rocks Could Sing: A Discovered Alphabet*

Author/Photographer Leslie McGuirk

Publishing Company/Date Tricycle Press/2011

ISBN# 978-1-582463704

Summary The stars of this book are the intriguing rocks found by the author along long stretches of beach. Not only are there rocks in the shapes of all of the letters, but there are also some in the shapes of animals and numbers. Photographed simply, these rocks form compositions that present not only the alphabet, but also the fascinating beauty created by nature's erosion. Each letter is introduced in the rock form and then used in printed form in a word associated with that letter.

Grades Pre-K–2

Content Area Fine Arts

Instructional Value Observation and perception

Text Structure Hidden Letter

Title *When Royals Wore Ruffles: A Funny and Fashionable Alphabet!*

Author Chesley McLaren and Pamela Jaber

Illustrator Chesley McLaren

Publishing Company/Date Schwartz & Wade Books/2009

ISBN# 978-0-375851667

Summary This high-energy alphabetic fashion show spotlights crazy fashion trends from Cleopatra to the modern day. Supercharged gouache and India ink illustrations playfully exaggerate each fashion whim. Hand-drawn, ornamental featured letters are capitalized and associated with a fashion term; hairstyles, hats, makeup, shoes, and undergarments are all part of the lineup. Several short paragraphs offer an explanation of the term and fun jargon, like LBD (little black dress), or fun facts, such as that hats in the Middle Ages were so tall that ladies had to have servants stand behind them to keep their hats on their heads.

Grades 3–6

Content Area Language Arts

Instructional Value Descriptive writing; vocabulary

Text Structure Conceptual text

Title *The Graphic Alphabet*

Author/Illustrator David Pelletier

Publishing Company/Date Orchard/1996

ISBN# 978-0-531-36001-9

Summary Set within a glossy black square, each letter is presented in either lowercase or uppercase. Instead of having their traditional shapes, the letters are ingeniously modified to depict their associated word. The H is associated with the word "hover," so the H seems to hover in the upper corner of the black square. The W (for "web") forms part of a spiderweb. The designs are sleek and sophisticated and invite readers to linger on each page.

Caldecott Honor Book

Grades All ages

Content Area Fine Arts

Instructional Value Graphic design; observation and perception

Text Structure Hidden letters

Title *Eight Hands Round: A Patchwork Alphabet*

Author Ann Whitford Paul

Illustrator Jeanette Winter

Publishing Company/Date HarperCollins/1996

ISBN# 978-0064434645

Summary Twenty-six lovely quilt patterns are organized alphabetically by pattern name. Each pattern name begins with an oversized capital letter, and the text pulls the reader back in time by speculating as to where the pattern name might have originated. A colorful detail of the pattern block next to a miniature quilt made of just those blocks shows how a simple pattern, multiplied, makes for a visual feast. Above the paragraph text is a vignette of country life in early America (a buggy ride, churning butter, or building a log cabin). Similar colors are used for the quilt and the vignette to further make the connection.

Grades 3–6
Content Area Mathematics and Social Studies
Instructional Value Geometry and measurement; history
Text Structure Single letter (expanded)

Title *3-D ABC: A Sculptural Alphabet*
Author/Illustrator Bob Raczka
Publishing Company/Date Millbrook Press/2007
ISBN# 978-0761394563
Summary Each beautifully photographed and mostly large-scale 20th-century sculpture is associated with a capital letter. The associated word is a descriptive reference to the sculpture, and the accompanying phrase offers an imaginative observation or suggestion on how to gain a deeper understanding of the sculpture. A full museum description, including artist, date, and location, is at the bottom of the page. Both indoor and outdoor pieces are included, as well as works created from a variety of materials including wood, stone, and even everyday objects.

Grades 3–6
Content Area Fine Art and Language Arts
Instructional Value Observation and perception; descriptive writing
Text Structure Single letter (expanded)

Title *The Hidden Alphabet*
Author/Illustrator Laura Vaccaro Seeger
Publishing Company/Date Roaring Book Press/2003
ISBN# 978-0761319412
Summary In this clever and interactive book, a thick black frame can be lifted to fully reveal the colorful art underneath. When the frame is lifted, the object that was initially framed now becomes an integral part of the letter. For example, an arrowhead is seen immediately in the center of the frame, but when the frame is lifted, the arrowhead is the center of the letter A. A single word is printed in white lowercase letters on the frame. This book is a visual delight, stimulating the mind through changing perspectives and by working from the part to the whole. Many of the letters revealed under the flaps are not completely conventional in shape; for example, the jigsaw puzzle piece associated with J takes a few extra notches out of the curve of the J.

Grades Pre-K–2

Content Area Fine Arts
Instructional Value Observation and perception
Text Structure Hidden letter

Title *Paul Thurlby's Alphabet*
Author/Illustrator Paul Thurlby
Publishing Company/Date Templar Books/2011
ISBN# 978-0763655655
Summary The graphic illustrations are in a vintage style where even the pages look as if they have been creased or aged in some manner. Each letter is simply presented in both capital and lowercase form on the left page of the spread, with the right page showing the letter taking on the shape of the object or vice versa. For example, the letter C becomes the arms that catch the soccer ball, and the letter R becomes a stylized seated rabbit.
Grades Pre-K–2
Content Area Fine Arts
Instructional Value Graphic design
Text Structure Hidden letter

Title *The ABC Book of American Homes*
Author Michael Shoulders
Illustrator Sarah S. Brannen
Publishing Company/Date Charlesbridge/2008
ISBN# 978-1570915659
Summary This is a survey of the many forms of shelter found in America over the last 300 years. Carefully executed watercolor illustrations show the architectural details that are attributed to each distinct style. Capital letters begin each paragraph, which clearly describes the architectural style and who might be living there. The styles include apartment, beach house, Cajun cottage, dome home, and yurt. All of the homes are depicted as cozy and warm places to live.
Grades 3–6
Content Area Social Studies
Instructional Value Culture
Text Structure Conceptual text

Careers

Title *LMNO Peas*
Author/Illustrator Keith Baker
Publishing Company/Date Beach Lane Books/2014
ISBN# 978-1416991410

Summary These charming and active peas (notice the title of the book) roll through the alphabet, highlighting many wonderful interests, hobbies, and careers. From acrobats, artists, and astronauts to gardeners, gigglers, and givers, to yogis and zoologists, this book gives the sense that the world is open and welcoming for anyone to do or try anything. A large, colorful capital letter is in the center of each illustration, on which the tiny peas are depicted in action, like kayaking down the letter K. Short phrases describe the action, and the author invites readers to consider, "Who are you?" at the end of the book.
Grades Pre-K–2
Content Area Language Arts
Instructional Value Phonemic awareness
Text Structure Single letter (expanded)

Title *Alpha Bravo Charlie: The Military Alphabet*
Author/Illustrator Chris L. Demarest
Publishing Company/Date Margaret K. McElderry Books/2005
ISBN# 978-0689869280
Summary This book combines several types of alphabets. In an upper corner of each page is a word that represents a letter in the International Communications Alphabet (ICA) utilized by the U.S. military. This is paired with a signal flag from the U.S. Navy. Powerful illustrations feature a military plane, ship, or other vehicle whose name begins with the featured letter, which appears in both uppercase and lowercase form. The pounding waves, the blasts from the helicopter blades, and the heat from the desert sand make for dynamic backdrops and a tribute to these brave men and women. The overall feeling is one of strength, precision, and cooperation among military personnel.
Grades Pre-K–2 and 3–6
Content Area Social Studies
Instructional Value Culture; history
Text Structure Conceptual Text

Title *Firefighters A to Z*
Author/Illustrator Chris L. Demarest
Publishing Company/Date Margaret K. McElderry Books/2000
ISBN# 978-0689837982
Summary Through richly colored, dramatic illustrations, this alphabetical understanding of the experiences, tools, and efforts of firemen comes to life. Each capital letter is associated with a word related to firefighting, and each spread offers a simple two-sentence rhyme connecting the featured words. "S is for Sounding. We test for weak zones. T is for Teamwork. No one works alone." The language is simple and informative, and the illustrations truly convey the details and actions of experienced firefighters.
Grades Pre-K–2
Content Area Social Studies

Instructional Value Culture
Text Structure Single letter (expanded)

Title *Country Road ABC: An Illustrated Journey through America's Farmland*
Author/Illustrator Authur Geisert
Publishing Company/Date Houghton Mifflin Books for Children/2010
ISBN# 978-0547194691
Summary Contemporary farm life is shared through sweeping panoramic scenes as well as detailed vignettes that capture rural beauty and cooperation among families to get the work done. These lovely color etchings have an atmospheric, somewhat nostalgic quality. Each capital letter is associated with a word or phrase (such as "ammonia fertilizer," "barn cats," "oat delivery," and "z-brace") that gives a sense of what everyday farm operation entails. A glossary provides further explanation for many terms.
Grades Pre-K–2
Content Area Social Studies
Instructional Value Culture; geography
Text Structure Single letter

Title Work: *An Occupational ABC*
Author/Illustrator Kellen Hatanaka
Publishing Company/Date Groundwood Books/2014
ISBN# 978-1554984091
Summary The alphabet is presented as a grouping of 26 adventurous and interesting occupations, from aviator to lumberjack to zookeeper. Each capital letter is placed, oversized, in the illustration as a silent but integral part of the story. The G serves as the back wall and ledge of the grocer's stand. The U supports the scoreboard for the umpire. The stylized illustrations include portly figures with minimal facial details who are shown using the basic tools associated with their trade. Only the name of the occupation appears. A soft, muted tone on a white background unifies the design and allows the essential message about the occupation to pop.
Grades Pre-K–2
Content Area Social Studies
Instructional Value Culture
Text Structure Single letter

Title *ABC Doctor: Staying Healthy from A to Z*
Author/Illustrator Liz Murphy
Publishing Company/Date Blue Apple Books/2012
ISBN# 978-1609053192
Summary A lovely, calming book for any child nervous about going to the doctor. Medical terminology like "appointment," "bandage," and "checkup" sets the tone for a pleasant

and helpful visit to the doctor. More advanced vocabulary like "otoscope," "reflex hammer," and "urine sample" is simply explained. The mixed media illustrations are friendly and cheerful, and both doctor and patient are usually smiling unless they are feeling ill. The capital letters are bold and colorful.

Grades Pre-K–2

Content Area Science

Instructional Value Life science

Text Structure Single letter (expanded)

Title *M Is for Money: An Economics Alphabet*

Author Debbie and Michael Shoulders

Illustrator Marty Kelley

Publishing Company/Date Sleeping Bear Press/2015

ISBN# 978-1585368174

Summary Economics terms and principles, including "abundance," "free markets," "goods and services," "jobs," "loans," "needs and wants," "resources," and "value," are presented from the point of view of elementary-school children. Lemonade stands, borrowing from your sister, trading lunch items, and doing chores for pay are among the ways these diverse and eager kids interact. The capital letter begins a short poem, and a side panel explains the concept in more detail. The watercolor illustrations are friendly and energetic.

Topic History

Grades 3–6

Content Area Language Arts and Social Studies

Instructional Value Rhyme and rhythm; history

Text Structure Conceptual text

Title *ABC Dentist*

Author Harriet Ziefert

Illustrator Liz Murphy

Publishing Company/Date Blue Apple Books/2012

ISBN# 978-1609053208

Summary This book will help soothe the anxious dental patient or inform a young person interested in the medical field. With clear and detailed explanations, a trip to the dentist and good dental health are broken down into 26 important elements (including "appointment," "cavity," "dental chair," and "zillion times cleaner"). Each capital letter is created from a bold swatch of fabric. The illustrations and collage elements are friendly and engaging. Both patient and doctor are smiling and focused on healthy teeth and a pleasant experience.

Grades Pre-K–2

Content Area Science

Instructional Value Life science

Text Structure Single letter (expanded)

Title *Lights on Broadway: A Theatrical Tour from A to Z*
Author Harriet Ziefert
Illustrator Elliot Kreloff
Publishing Company/Date Blue Apple Books/2009
ISBN# 978-1934706688
Summary An insider's guide to all things theater, this book is packed with inspiring quotes from stage actors and definitions for a variety of words, phrases, and expressions used both onstage and off (including "audition," "grip," "rehearsal," and "understudy"). The excitement and sparkle begin with the glitter-laden lettering of the front cover and continue even after the book is read, with a CD in the back. The featured letter is capitalized and repeated in a variety of typefaces in the words associated with that letter. The use of collage and retro-style cartoon characters helps to bring the energy of the stage to each page.
Grades 7–12
Content Area Language Arts
Instructional Value Descriptive writing
Text Structure Conceptual text

Children

Title *M Is for Mischief: An A to Z of Naughty Children*
Author Linda Ashman
Illustrator Nancy Carpenter
Publishing Company/Date Dutton's Children's Books/2008
ISBN# 978-0525475644
Summary A warning at the beginning of the book alerts readers that they will see and read about obnoxious children and that any further reading is at their own risk! The following pages showcase 26 of the most wild, careless, and unpleasant children, who are sure to remind the young reader what not to do—from Angry Abby to Eavesdropping Eva to Zany Zelda. Hand-drawn capital letters begin the alliterative poems of roughly 20 words each. Energetic illustrations share the intensity of emotion or action, and the collage elements are a fun way to add more reality.
Grades Pre-K–2 and 3–6
Content Area Language Arts
Instructional Value Alliteration; rhyme and rhythm; vocabulary
Text Structure Single letter (expanded)

Title *Augie to Zebra: An Alphabet Book!*
Author Caspar Babypants
Illustrator Kate Endle
Publishing Company/Date Sasquatch Books/2012
ISBN# 978-1570617508

Summary Each collage illustration is created from beautiful papers and presents a child from around the world interacting with nature or with animals, or in play. The letters are in uppercase and lowercase and are used in alliterative sentences. Children will enjoy searching within the composition for other items beginning with the letter of the page. A key in the back of the book lists these items and ensures that none of these hidden gems are missed.
Grades Pre-K–2
Content Area Language Arts
Instructional Value Alliteration; phonemic awareness
Text Structure Single letter (expanded)

Title: *ABC Kids*
Author/Illustrator: Simon Basher
Publishing Company/Date: Kingfisher/2011
ISBN# 978-0753464953
Summary: Japanese-style graphics illustrate children playfully interacting with animals and enjoying food. Each letter is presented in both uppercase and lowercase and is repeated in a tongue-twister of usually five words. The entire lowercase alphabet is printed along the bottom of each spread, with the featured letter of that page underlined, allowing children to keep track of the position of the letter within the alphabet.
Grades Pre-K–2
Content Area Language Arts
Instructional Value Alliteration; alphabetic principle; phonemic awareness
Text Structure Single letter (expanded)

Title *AlphaBest: The Zany, Zanier, Zaniest Book about Comparatives and Superlatives*
Author Helaine Becker
Illustrator Dave Whamond
Publishing Company/Date Kids Can Press/2012
ISBN# 978-1554537150
Summary The brave, braver, bravest hero combats the angry, angrier, angriest prankster in an amusement park on the zany, zanier, zaniest day. Every letter is associated with an adjective written in its basic form, followed by a comparative and then a superlative. The energetic cartoon drawings evoke a busy Saturday-morning cartoon. A guide in the back of the book provides an aid to teachers and a grammar lesson on how to form comparatives and superlatives.
Grades Pre-K–2 and 3–6
Content Area Language Arts
Instructional Value Descriptive writing; grammar
Text Structure Single letter (expanded)

Title *An Annoying ABC*
Author Barbara Bottner
Illustrator Michael Emberley
Publishing Company/Date Knopf Books for Young Readers/2011
ISBN# 978-037596708-5
Summary A quiet morning in a preschool class of children, whose names each begin with a letter of the alphabet, is interrupted as a domino chain of alphabetical unfriendly acts occur. "Adelaide annoyed Bailey. Bailey blamed Clyde." But later, when Adelaide apologizes, another domino effect occurs, this time without words and in illustration only, setting all of the wrongs straight again. The pencil and watercolor illustrations capture the action and spunk of these diverse youngsters and their busy learning environment. Each uppercase letter that starts the name of the child is set on a different square of color.
Grades Pre-K–2
Content Area Language Arts
Instructional Value Alliteration; vocabulary
Text Structure Single letter (expanded)

Title *Sleepy ABC*
Author Margaret Wise Brown
Illustrator Karen Katz
Publishing Company/Date Harper/2009
ISBN# 978-0061288630
Summary From the author of *Goodnight Moon*, this book shares 26 ways that people and animals wind down the day. Simple and soothing sentences form gentle rhymes like "A is for Aaaah when a small kitten sighs" and "B is for Baaa when the lambs close their eyes." Other topic words include "dreams," "kissing," "pillow," "quiet," and "zipper." The featured letter stands out, as it is capitalized, colorful, and placed in a frame of contrasting color. The painted collage illustrations are sweet, with polka-dot backgrounds and friendly colors. Children have large, round faces and tiny facial features; all are smiling and peaceful.
Grades Pre-K–2
Content Area Language Arts
Instructional Value Phonemic awareness; rhyme and rhythm
Text Structure Single letter (expanded)

Title *Matthew A.B.C.*
Author/Illustrator Peter Catalanotto
Publishing Company/Date Atheneum Books for Young Readers/2002
ISBN# 978-0689845826
Summary Mrs. Tuttle's kindergarten class includes 25 boys named Matthew; luckily their last names begin with different letters of the alphabet. The featured letter also begins a

word that can be used to describe that student. Matthew A. is extremely affectionate, and Matthew B. loves Band-Aids, while Matthew G. has trouble with glue. The letters of the alphabet are presented in both uppercase and lowercase. The newest Matthew is presented at the end of the book and fits in in his own unique way. An observant reader may notice that the friendly cowlicks of Matthew C. spell "hello." The autumnal palette of the illustrations lend to the warm and inviting feeling of the book.

Grades Pre-K–2
Content Area Language Arts
Instructional Value Alphabetic principle
Text Structure Single letter (expanded)

Title *Gyo Fujikawa's A to Z Picture Book*
Author/ Illustrator Gyo Fujikawa
Publishing Company/Date Sterling Publishing Company Inc./2010
ISBN# 978-1402768187
Summary Alternating between spreads of black and white and those with color, Fujikawa introduces every letter on the black-and-white page with a capital letter in an upper corner and a lowercase letter in the bottom corner. Filling the page are examples of mostly nouns (but also some verbs) beginning with that letter, illustrated in pen and ink. The varying scale adds to the visual interest and assures that this book cannot be rushed through. In the color spreads, adorable, happy children of varying nationalities charmingly cuddle and sweetly observe their natural surroundings. Even the witch and the monsters are disarmed by the children and become part of the essential balance of the book.

Grades Pre-K–2
Content Area Language Arts
Instructional Value Phonemic awareness; vocabulary
Text Structure Single letter

Title *D Is for Dress-Up: The ABC's of What We Wear*
Author/Illustrator Maria Carluccio
Publishing Company/Date Chronicle Books/2016
ISBN# 978-1452140254
Summary Children of various ethnic backgrounds play dress-up. Some wear costumes for Halloween, another wears an apron and cooks, two friends wear T-shirts at the beach, and others wear ice skates. The scenes are a mixture of outdoor and indoor ones and take place during a variety of seasons. The illustrations offer interesting textures and patterns and have a palette of soft colors. The capital letter is shown above the target word. Among the target words are "costumes," "ensemble," "fabric," "jeans," "knits," and "yoga pants."

Grades Pre-K–2

Content Area Language Arts
Instructional Value Vocabulary
Text Structure Single letter

Title *ABC School's for Me!*
Author Susan B. Katz
Illustrator Lynn Munsinger
Publishing Company/Date Scholastic Press/2015
ISBN# 978-0545530927
Summary A classroom of young bears enjoy a day of kindergarten where each activity is connected to a letter of the alphabet. The capital letter begins the phrase, and many of the phrases form a gentle rhyme. "Books that are just right for me. Crayons for coloring, in my hand. Dump trucks, playing in the sand." The watercolor and pen-and-ink illustrations are detailed and colorful, making these bears especially fuzzy and cuddly. The joy of school and the creative learning opportunities are emphasized.
Grades Pre-K–2
Content Area Language Arts
Instructional Value Alphabetic principle
Text Structure Single letter (expanded)

Title *Alice and Aldo*
Author/Illustrator Alison Lester
Publishing Company/Date Walter Lorraine Books/1998
ISBN# 978-0395870921
Summary Alice and her adorable stuffed donkey wake up and spend the day doing many familiar things, from having breakfast in bed, to getting clothes from the closet, to helping Dad do the dishes. Each of the detailed watercolor with pen-and-ink illustrations is set in a frame of sometimes a dozen or so items that also begin with the featured letter. Many of the colorful scenes are outdoors, where Alice "runs down a rabbit" or "sing[s] in the sandbox." The letter appears only in lowercase at the beginning of the featured words.
Grades Pre-K–2
Content Area Language Arts
Instructional Value Phonemic awareness
Text Structure Single letter (expanded)

Title *Annie, Bea, and Chi Chi Dolores: A School Day Alphabet*
Author Donna Maurer
Illustrator Denys Cazet
Publishing Company/Date Orchard Books/1993
ISBN# 978-0531086179

Summary Three animal friends (a bear, a dog, and a hippopotamus) spend a day together in kindergarten, from the bus ride to school, through all the activities, to preparing to head home. A single word or phrase is given for each letter of the alphabet. The letters are presented in capital and lowercase. The drawings are charming and show the easy, happy camaraderie of the main characters. Many of the fun opportunities in kindergarten, like drawing, follow-the-leader, giggling, and snack time, are highlighted.
Grades Pre-K–2
Content Area Language Arts
Instructional Value Alphabetic principle
Text Structure Single letter

Title *A Child's Day: An Alphabet of Play*
Author/Illustrator Ida Pearle
Publishing Company/Date Harcourt Children's Books/2008
ISBN# 978-0152065522
Summary Each page displays an uppercase and lowercase letter paired with a verb associated with play. Colorful paper-collage illustrations composed with beautiful papers show each child engaged in play. Readers are invited to look for the simple opportunities around them to "Catch," "Dance," and "Whistle." The simplicity of message pairs well with the simplicity of illustration.
Grades Pre-K–2
Content Area Language Arts
Instructional Value Alphabetic principle
Text Structure Single letter

Title *ABCers*
Author Carole Lexa Schaefer
Illustrator Pierr Morgan
Publishing Company/Date Viking Books for Young Readers/2012
ISBN# 978-0670012312
Summary A diverse group of children gather outside their apartment building on a summer afternoon and set out for some fun in the park. Each capital letter of the alphabet is in a bold color and begins a simple phrase, such as "A is for Arm linkers" and "G is for Giggle givers" The joy with which they dance, jump, and tiptoe is evidenced by their wide smiles. Soft pastel colors provide a friendly, cheerful backdrop for these active friends. The endpapers provide a map of the city neighborhood so readers can trace the trail of the alphabet letters and the location of each activity.
Grades Pre-K–2
Content Area Language Arts
Instructional Value Vocabulary
Text Structure Single letter (expanded)

Title *The Sleepy Little Alphabet: A Bedtime Story from Alphabet Town*
Author Judy Sierra
Illustrator Melissa Sweet
Publishing Company/Date Knopf Books for Young Readers/2009
ISBN# 978-0375940026
Summary It's sleepytime in Alphabet Town, where adult capital letters try to get their wide-eyed lowercase-letter children to go to bed. The letters within the charming pencil and watercolor illustrations are given facial features and fun personalities and are depicted riding a bike, jumping on the bed, and drawing, among other things. The narrative includes lowercase letters that are bold within the text: "q is quiet as a bunny. r and s read something funny."
Grades Pre-K–2
Content Area Language Arts
Instructional Value Phonemic awareness; rhyme and rhythm
Text Structure Hidden letter

Classic Characters

Title *Thomas's ABC Book*
Author Rev. W. Awdry
Photographer Kenny McArthur, David Mitton, and Terry Permane
Publishing Company/Date Random House/2010
ISBN# 978-0679893578
Summary Thomas the Tank Engine and his many friends, including Bertie, Diesel, and Henry, as well as simple train-related words such as "all aboard," "tracks," and "up," form an alphabet. Photographs show these hardworking trains in action and their camaraderie. The capitalized featured letter is in a colorful boldface type. Above the photograph is a simple association ("E is for Edward"), and below the photograph is a short sentence ("Edward, a kind engine, helps everyone").
Grades Pre-K–2
Content Area Language Arts
Instructional Value Alphabetic principle
Text Structure Single letter (expanded)

Title *Babar's ABC*
Author/Illustrator Laurent de Brunhoff
Publishing Company/Date Harry N. Abrams/2012
ISBN# 978-1419703829
Summary The much-loved characters of Babar, Celeste, and their friends are represented doing a variety of activities throughout their town of Celesteville. The uppercase and lowercase letters are in block form in an upper corner and then associated with a noun,

which is the subject of the main illustration. The words that start with the letter are in boldface. One or two framed illustrative inserts add additional uses of the letter through sentences like "A frog plays a flute in the flower garden."

Grades Pre-K–2

Content Area Language Arts

Instructional Value Phonemic awareness

Text Structure Single letter

Title *The Alphabet Book*

Author/Illustrator P. D. Eastman

Publishing Company/Date Random House Books for Young Readers/2015

ISBN# 978-0553511116

Summary Each letter is presented in capital form in an upper corner and highlighted within the alphabet column that runs along the right side, so that readers can see the letter's position within the alphabet. The letters are associated with a two- or three-word phrase usually describing an animal next to, on top of, or holding an object. "Bird on bike" is the phrase for B, and "Octopus with oars" is the phrase for O. The colorful cartoon illustrations with expressive eyes are humorous and playful and show some animals wearing clothes, playing the guitar, or typing on a typewriter, among other things.

Grades Pre-K–2

Content Area Language Arts

Instructional Value Phonemic awareness

Text Structure Single letter

Title *R Is for Rocket: An ABC Book*

Author/Illustrator Tad Hills

Publishing Company/Date Schwartz & Wade Books/2015

ISBN# 978-0553522280

Summary Children are invited to learn with Rocket the dog and his group of animal friends. From finding acorns while an owl draws an angry alligator to Bella balancing on a ball while a big blue butterfly watches, this book offers plenty of simple and fun words beginning with each letter of the alphabet. The oil and color pencil illustrations are delightfully sweet, and the alliterative sentences are warm and engaging. The book concludes with the sentence, "Ah, the wondrous, mighty, gorgeous alphabet."

Grades Pre-K–2

Content Area Language Arts

Instructional Value Alliteration

Text Structure Single letter (expanded)

Title *Puddle's ABC*

Author/Illustrator Holly Hobbie

Publishing Company/Date Little, Brown and Company/2000

ISBN# 978-0316365932

Summary Puddle the pig teaches his friend Otto the turtle the letters of the alphabet so that Otto can learn to write his name. This short storyline is the framework for Puddle's creative presentation of the alphabet. Watercolor illustrations convey the artistic energy and gentle humor of the pig, who himself draws pictures for each letter. Each letter is presented in uppercase and lowercase and associated with a short alliterative phrase, such as "Ant alone with apple," "Ballerina blowing bubbles," or "Crocodile crunching carrots."

Grades Pre-K–2

Content Area Language Arts

Instructional Value Alliteration

Text Structure Single letter (expanded)

Title *Alfie's ABC*

Author/Illustrator Shirley Hughes

Publishing Company/Date Lothrop, Lee & Shepard Books/1998

ISBN# 978-0688161262

Summary Four-year-old Alfie and his little sister Annie Rose engage in play and interact with neighbors and relatives in this charming and tender book. The letters are clearly presented in capital and lowercase and then again in capital form at the beginning of a simple sentence, such as "B is for bedtime and blanket" or "C is for Chessie, Alfie's black-and-white cat." The enjoyment of play and the warmth of family are evident in each of the finely detailed watercolor illustrations, which are full of delightful details offering young readers many moments of discovery.

Grades Pre-K–2

Content Area Language Arts

Instructional Value Alliteration; phonemic awareness

Text Structure Single letter (expanded)

Title *Goodnight Moon ABC: An Alphabet Book*

Author/Illustrator Clement Hurd (based on the book by Margaret Wise Brown)

Publishing Company/Date Harper/2010

ISBN# 978-0061894848

Summary The familiar items from *Goodnight Moon* become the focus words for each letter of the alphabet. Next to each uppercase and lowercase letter is the word for the object and then an illustration of the object itself. Some pages have just one object, and others have several. A colorful spread of the entire room appears for the letter I ("In the great green room") and again for Z ("Zzzz Goodnight noises everywhere") Objects include "air," "brush," "lamp," and "red balloon."

Grades Pre-K–2

Content Area Language Arts

Instructional Value Alphabetic principle; phonemic awareness

Text Structure Single Letter

Title *Kipper's A to Z: An Alphabet Adventure*
Author/Illustrator Mick Inkpen
Publishing Company/Date HMH Books for Young Readers/201
ISBN# 978-0152025946
Summary Kipper and Arnold first notice an ant, and then they follow the bumblebee that
leads them to a caterpillar, and so on. The uppercase and lowercase letters are presented,
and the featured word is in boldface. The alphabetic storyline continues throughout the
book, while the zebra keeps checking in to see when he can appear. The art is charming
and sweet. Kids will find it amusing to follow the meandering adventures of Kipper and
his friend.
Grades Pre-K–2
Content Area Language Arts
Instructional Value Alphabetic principle
Text Structure Single letter (expanded)

Title *Miss Spider's ABC*
Author/Illustrator David Kirk
Publishing Company/Date Scholastic Press/1998
ISBN# 978-0590282796
Summary All of the alphabetical insect friends of Miss Spider gather and prepare a surprise
for her birthday. The capital letters are paired with a short, often alliterative and poetic
phrase, from "Ants await" to "Bumblebees blow balloons" and "Yellow jackets yield
to the zebra butterfly." The illustrations seem to glow and shimmer and are saturated
with rich color and enhanced with subtle shading. There is a sense of eager anticipation
among the insects. The lush, jungle-like background further adds to the sense of magic.
Grades Pre-K–2
Content Area Language Arts
Instructional Value Alliteration
Text Structure Single letter (expanded)

Title *The Three Bears ABC*
Author Grace Maccarone
Illustrator Hollie Hibbert
Publishing Company/Date Albert Whitman & Company/2013
ISBN# 978-0807579046
Summary This familiar story fits neatly into the framework of the alphabet: B is for "bears,"
G is for a "girl" and J is for "just right." The story keeps an upbeat pace, with the capi-
talized featured letter beginning the several lines of text. Vibrant-colored illustrations
capture the emotions in this charming story, the many cozy details in the bears' house,
and the lush forest that surrounds them.
Grades Pre-K–2

Content Area Language Arts
Instructional Value Alphabetic principle
Text Structure Single letter (expanded)

Title *Superhero ABC*
Author/Illustrator Bob McLeod
Publishing Company/Date HarperCollins Children's Books/2006
ISBN# 978-0060745158
Summary For the youngest comic book fans, this alphabetic array of male and female superheroes delivers a punch. Eye-popping illustrations, alliterative rhymes, and bubble-outlined dialogue showcase fascinating superheroes including Astor-Man, who is always alert for an alien attack, and Ms. Incredible, who becomes invisible in an instant. The letters are presented in uppercase and lowercase and appear in a dozen other words to complete the description of each uniquely amazing superhero.
Grades 3–6
Content Area Language Arts
Instructional Value Alliteration; vocabulary
Text Structure Single letter (expanded)

Title *Fancy Nancy's Favorite Fancy Words: From Accessories to Zany*
Author Jane O'Connor
Illustrator Robin Preiss Glasser
Publishing Company/Date HarperCollins/2008
ISBN# 978-0061549236
Summary The sparkles on the cover set the tone for Fancy Nancy, a girl who loves all things fancy. In this book she shares a fancy word for each letter of the alphabet. The first letter of the word is capitalized and boldface. This book is a true vocabulary builder, as each word is defined and then used in a sentence that describes the scene illustrated. From carrying an enormous armload of "accessories" to "ooh la la," the pen-and-ink over watercolor illustrations are as imaginative, joyous, and zany as Nancy herself.
Grades Pre-K–2
Content Area Language Arts
Instructional Value Vocabulary
Text Structure Single letter (expanded)

Title *Curious George Learns the Alphabet*
Author/Illustrator H. A. Rey
Publishing Company/Date Houghton Mifflin Company/2013
ISBN# 978-0544105232
Summary The adorable monkey George learns the alphabet through the drawings of his friend, the man with the yellow hat. The text is clear and repetitive and highlights a

series of words that begin with the featured letter. Spreads shows a capital and a lowercase letter paired with a featured word. The illustrations further connect the letter with the word by incorporating the boldface letter within the illustration. The capital A forms the jaws of the alligator, and the lowercase A forms a frame around the apple. The charm of these characters and the strong object examples selected for each letter are timeless.

Grades Pre-K–2

Content Area Language Arts

Instructional Value Alphabetic principle; phonemic awareness

Text Structure Hidden letter

Title *Richard Scarry's ABC Word Book*

Author/Illustrator Richard Scarry

Publishing Company/Date Sterling Publishing Co./2011

ISBN# 978-1402772214

Summary The delightful anthropomorphic animal characters of Busytown offer loads of examples of alphabetic objects and activities. The letters are presented in capital and lowercase form in the upper left corner, and every occurrence of the letter is highlighted in red in the largely alliterative text. The colorful images, with their fine black outlines, detail the numerous examples of words associated with a letter. Other Richard Scarry alphabet books include *Richard Scarry Mr. Paint Pig's ABC's* (2013).

Grades Pre-K–2

Content Area Language Arts

Instructional Value Alphabetic principle; phonemic awareness

Text Structure Single letter (expanded)

Title *Alligators All Around*

Author/Illustrator Maurice Sendak

Publishing Company/Date HarperCollins/1991

ISBN# 978-0064432542

Summary This proud alligator family is active and a bit mischievous. Whether they are "bursting balloons," "getting giggles," or "riding reindeer," they are "never napping." Often dressed in feathered hats, carrying umbrellas, or wearing ties, this alligator family's antics are engaging. The alphabet letter is in bold uppercase and followed by a simple descriptive phase. The short phrases make for a fun and charming rhythmic read.

Grades Pre-K–2

Content Area Language Arts

Instructional Value Alliteration

Text Structure Single letter

Title *Miss Bindergarten Gets Ready for Kindergarten*

Author Joseph Slate

Illustrator Ashley Wolff

Publishing Company/Date Dutton Children's Books/1996

ISBN# 978-0525454465

Summary This book could help relieve any anxiety a new kindergarten student might have. With warm, cheerful illustrations, each letter is matched to a student's name and an animal. Fran Lester is a frog, and Sara von Hoff is a squirrel. The snappy rhyming sentences create an upbeat tone. Between alternating spreads of children are spreads of the loving preparations of Miss Bindergarten. In the final pages, the numerous activities of kindergarten are illustrated. A yearbook-like depiction of each student, with his or her name and associated animal, is also in the back. The same cast of characters takes a field trip in *Miss Bindergarten Takes a Field Trip* (2001).

Grades Pre-K–2

Content Area Language Arts

Instructional Value Rhyme and rhythm

Text Structure Single letter (expanded)

Title *Max's ABC*

Author/Illustrator Rosemary Wells

Publishing Company/Date Viking/2006

ISBN# 978-0670060740

Summary The bunny siblings Max and Ruby work together to deal with some hungry ants that discover all kinds of goodies spilled on Max's shirt or left in his pockets. Ruby works to get rid of the ants, but it is Max who returns them to their ant farm. Each bold capital letter is prominently anchored in a top corner of the page, and every time the featured letter is used in a sentence, it is in boldface. The storyline is simple and engaging, and children will relate to the sticky spills that Max creates. The drawings are expressive and are set on a variety of energetic and boldly colored backgrounds.

Grades Pre-K–2

Content Area Language Arts

Instructional Value Phonemic awareness

Text Structure Single letter (expanded)

Fantasy

Title *Animalia*

Author/Illustrator Graeme Base

Publishing Company/Date Harry N. Abrams, Inc./1993

ISBN# 978-0810919396

Summary In this superbly and elaborately illustrated book, each page dives into a world of creative detail and richness within a magical fantasyland. An alliterative phrase like "Great Green Gorillas Growing Grapes in a Gorgeous Glass Greenhouse" is presented in all capital letters. The illustrations not only capture the description but also have countless other references to the featured letter. In the case of G, depicted are a tiny gnome, a gecko, a guard, a gift, a goat, a pair of goggles, and many more items. Each reading will likely uncover new delights. The typeface varies to further illustrate the topic or mood, making each letter panel unique.

Grades 3–6

Content Area Fine Arts and Language Arts

Instructional Value Observation and perception; alliteration

Text Structure Single letter (expanded)

Title *G Is for One Gzonk! An Alpha-Number-Bet Book*

Author/Illustrator Tony DiTerlizzi

Publishing Company/Date Simon and Schuster/2006

ISBN# 978-0689852909

Summary In this Seuss-like world, a young boy creates his own illustrations for every letter of the alphabet. The illustrations are imaginative and include Angry Ack, a red, dinosaur-like creature that wears a gym sock on each ear and eats dirty clothes directly from the laundry hamper. Bloobytack, a blue, rabbit-like creature, collects all loose items from the floor and stacks them on its back. The letters are presented in capital and lowercase form in an upper corner. Other than the alliterative description of the creature, the remaining text is a humorously random wild ride.

Grades Pre-K–2

Content Area Language Arts

Instructional Value Alliteration; descriptive writing

Text Structure Single letter (expanded)

Title *Take Away the A*

Author Michaël Escoffier

Illustrator Kris Di Giacomo

Publishing Company/Date Enchanted Lion Books/2014

ISBN# 978-1592701568

Summary In this clever take on alphabet books, the featured letter is presented within a word, and then the letter is removed to form a new word. The transformations are humorous and sometimes surreal; for example, "Without the A the beast is the best," "Without the C the chair has hair," and "Without the Y the yours are ours." Each letter is presented in capital form. The playful narrative is overlaid on mixed-media illustrations, composed of cool colors, that have a childlike and charming quality.

Grades Pre-K–2

Content Area Language Arts

Instructional Value Phonemic awareness; rhyme and rhythm

Text Structure Single letter (expanded)

Title *The Dangerous Alphabet*

Author Neil Gaiman

Illustrator Gris Grimly

Publishing Company/Date HarperCollins/2008

ISBN# 978-0060783334

Summary This spine-chilling tale is of two Victorian children and their pet gazelle as they hunt for treasure through a darkly whimsical underground urban landscape filled with monsters and pirates. The letters of the alphabet are painted in capital form and refer to components of the story ("B is for Boat," "E is for Evil," "N is for Night"). The 13 rhyming couplets give a framework for the story, but the visual storytelling, with its gothic style and sepia tones, is complex and entertaining for both children and adults who appreciate the more ghastly. A warning to the purists: the letters W and V switch spots, and the letter C stands for "see" and the letter U for "you."

Grades 3–6

Content Area Language Arts

Instructional Value Descriptive writing

Text Structure Single letter (expanded)

Title *Dr. Seuss's ABC*

Author/Illustrator Theodor Seuss Geisel

Publishing Company/Date Random House/1991

ISBN# 978-0394800301

Summary With his signature imaginative style, Seuss's alphabet book parades a host of fun and unusual characters in the most fanciful situations. Every letter is shown in uppercase and lowercase form and then with a gentle rhyme composed of a string of words beginning with that letter. The pictures incorporate all of the elements in the text and bring the amusing situations to life. Children will enjoy repeating the text multiple times, especially the phrases they find funny.

Grades Pre-K–2

Content Area Language Arts

Instructional Value Alliteration; alphabetic principle

Text Structure Single letter (expanded)

Title: *The Gashlycrumb Tinies or, After the Outing*

Author /Illustrator Edward Gorey

Publishing Company/Date: Houghton Mifflin Harcourt Publishing Company/1997

ISBN# 978-0151003082

Summary In this dark but humorous book, each capital letter is presented and then begins the name of a child unwittingly done in by a random accident. Some of the accidents are of the everyday possibility, like "A is for Amy who fell down the stairs"; others are more fantastic, like "X is for Xerxes devoured by mice." The rhyming wit of the individual tragic tales is illustrated with densely crosshatched black-and-white pen-and-ink drawings.

Grades: 7–12

Content Area: Language Arts
Instructional Value Descriptive writing
Text Structure: Single letter (expanded)

Title *Ogres! Ogres Ogres! A Feasting Frenzy from A to Z*
Author Nicholas Heller
Illustrator Jos. A. Smith
Publishing Company/Date Greenwillow Books/1999
ISBN# 978-0688169862
Summary The reader is invited to peek into a basement where 26 playful and energetic ogres enjoy a massive alphabetical buffet. The joy of alliterative sentences is enhanced by the lengthy old-fashioned names of the silly ogres and the clever wordplay. Each alphabet letter begins an adjective, the name of an ogre, and a verb describing what it is doing. The noun that names the food the ogre is eating begins with the next letter in the alphabet; for example, "Buehlah blows bubbles in her chocolate" and "Pernilla is peppering her parsnip quiche." Each alphabet letter is presented in color at the beginning of the name of the ogre. The gouache and watercolor illustrations are charming and present these ogres as unique and quirky individuals who clearly have their own personal gastronomic tastes.
Grade Pre-K–2
Content Area Language Arts
Instructional Value Alliteration; phonemic awareness; vocabulary
Text Structure Single letter (expanded)

Title *Antics! An Alphabetical Anthology*
Author/Illustrator Cathy Hepworth
Publishing Company/Date G. P. Putnam's Sons/1992
ISBN# 978-0399218620
Summary This is a witty take on alphabet books, in which ants portray famous people or concepts, and where the featured word includes the word "ant" within it. The old lady ant with a silver bun sitting in her rocking chair and knitting on her front porch is "AnciANT." The mad scientist ant with his white lab coat and test tubes is "BrilliANT." Other clever word choices include "ImmigrANTs," "ObservANT," and "SANTa Claus." The softly textured colored pencil illustrations paired with each single word are detailed and expressive. The alphabet letter is presented only at the beginning of the featured word, in boldface and capitalized.
Grades All ages
Content Area Language Arts
Instructional Value Grammar
Text Structure Single letter

Title *An A To Z of Fairies*
Author Caroline Stills
Illustrator Heath McKenzie
Publishing Company/Date Little Hare/2011
ISBN# 978-1921714504
Summary Children who love the fantasy world of fairies, pixies, and changelings will be delighted with these bright, colorful cartoon illustrations where wide-eyed children encounter all sorts of mayhem. Each letter is presented in capital form and in the first letter of a word associated with the land of fairies. The four-lined ABCB rhyming scheme offers enough explanation necessary to understand the illustration. A purple, blue, and green fairy is on every page, adding a search-and-find element to the book. A key in the back of the book reveals each hidden location.
Grades 3–6
Content Area Language Arts
Instructional Value Rhyme and rhythm; vocabulary
Text Structure Single letter (expanded)

Title *An ABC of Pirates*
Author Caroline Stills
Illustrator Heath McKenzie
Publishing Company/Date Little Hare Books/2010
ISBN# 978-1921272776
Summary In the manner of Pippi Longstocking, children take on adult roles yet possess a magic, playful quality. Each letter stands for a pirate-related word and is used up to four times in a rhyming description of the page's action. Zebras, pizzas, and saxophones are among the animals and everyday objects familiar to children and illustrated in the detailed and active background. In addition to a glossary, the back of the book offers an additional experience in a section called "Did you find all of these objects in the pictures?" This list of roughly 300 words is organized alphabetically.
Grades 3–6
Content Area Language Arts
Instructional Value Rhyme and rhythm; vocabulary
Text Structure Single letter (expanded)

Title *The Z Was Zapped*
Author/Illustrator Chris van Allsburg
Publishing Company/Date Houghton Mifflin Company/1987
ISBN# 978-0395446126
Summary Each of the 26 acts in this theater performance showcases a letter on a curtained stage at a transformative moment. The letter A is pelted with rocks during an avalanche,

the letter B has a bite taken out of it, and so on through many dastardly acts of being cut, flattened, kidnapped, nailed, and zapped. The written description appears on the page following the illustration, creating suspense and allowing the reader a moment to guess what might have occurred. The detailed black-and-white drawings are dramatic and highly textured.

Grades All ages
Content Area Fine Arts
Instructional Value Observation and perception
Text Structure Single letter (expanded)

Title *The Ultimate Alphabet*
Author/Illustrator Mike Wilks
Publishing Company/Date Henry Holt and Co./1986
ISBN# 978-0805000764
Summary Twenty-six minutely detailed paintings capture nearly 8,000 objects, each associated with a letter of the alphabet. Each capital letter is followed by a listing of 20 or so items to be found in the painting, as well as an exact number of total items that can be found in the image. A guide in the back lists all of the items. The paintings are dreamlike, juxtaposing the expected with the unexpected, inviting viewers on a journey through this visual dictionary.

Grades 7–12
Content Area Fine Arts and Language Arts
Instructional Value Observation and perception; vocabulary
Text Structure Single letter (expanded)

Health and Activity

Title *Fed Up! A Feast of Frazzled Foods*
Author/Illustrator Rex Barron
Publishing Company/Date G. P. Putnam's Sons/2000
ISBN# 978-0399234507
Summary In this edgy and emotion-filled text, the moods of a host of colorful fruits and vegetables are explored as they contemplate their fate. The anxious apples leerily eye the discarded apple core; the cabbage sobs as it sees a container of coleslaw. The two- or three-word alliterative phrases identify the food and the action. Another example is "Dills Debate Destiny," where elderly pickles, dressed as if at a Roman forum, energetically debate an issue. The featured letter always appears in capital form and in boldface. The colored pencil illustrations are humorous and offer lots of detail to support the anthropomorphizing of these fruits and vegetables.

Grades Pre-K–2
Content Area Language Arts

Instructional Value Alliteration
Text Structure Single letter

Title *Bad Kitty*
Author/Illustrator Nick Bruel
Publishing Company/Date Roaring Book Press/2015
ISBN# 978-1626722453
Summary A kitty is horrified when presented only with healthy food options (asparagus, beets, and cauliflower) only to create alphabetical mayhem through the house ("ate my homework," "bit Grandma," "clawed the curtains"). When presented with a new alphabetical assortment of food (fried flies, nightingale nuggets, and yak yogurt), the kitty decides to be very good and, again through the alphabet, helps around the house ("apologized to Grandma," "bought me new toys," "cleaned her cat box"). Each of the four times a letter is presented, it is red, capitalized, and in boldface. The energy of the drawings focuses on the strong emotional reactions of the kitty.
Grades Pre-K–2
Content Area Language Arts
Instructional Value Vocabulary
Text Structure Single letter (expanded)

Title *A Is for Awesome*
Author/Illustrator Dallas Clayton
Publishing Company/Date Candlewick Press/2014
ISBN# 978-0763657451
Summary With a strong message of living life to its fullest, this feel-good book is full of big ideas. Each capital letter is linked to a word that is defined with a brief phrase. Several small illustrations of items starting with the focus letter encircle the text, which itself is hand-drawn to appear as if made from a soft, furry, colorful material. Entries include "B is for Beautiful Big Bold and Brazen," "D is for Dreaming things never expected," "G is for Greatness you're well on your way," and "V is for Values and keeping them true."
Grades 3–6
Content Area Language Arts
Instructional Value Vocabulary
Text Structure Single letter (expanded)

Title *P Is for Peloton: The A–Z of Cycling*
Author Suze Clemitson and Mark Fairhurst
Illustrator Mark Fairhurst
Publishing Company/Date Bloomsbury/2015
ISBN# 978-1472912855

Summary An inspiring and information-rich book for any avid cyclist or even those new to the sport. Each letter of the alphabet forms its own chapter and is associated with a dozen or so terms, stories about famous cyclists, and events. A is for "Arrivée," "Abandon," "Aerodynamics," "Allez," "Alpe D'huez," "Angliru," "Ardennes," and "Attack." The narrative clearly explains these words and includes loads of supporting details, from the amazing to the bizarre. The illustrations hark back to the graphic art deco posters of the 1930s.
Grades 7–12
Content Area Language Arts and Social Studies
Instructional Value Descriptive writing; history
Text Structure Conceptual text

Title *Adventurous to Zealous: All About Me from A to Z*
Author/Photographer Colleen Dolphin
Publishing Company/Date ABDO Publishing Company/2009
ISBN# 978-1604534900
Summary This book presents the alphabet in both uppercase and lowercase and features adjectives that describe both positive and negative qualities. The negative qualities include "lazy," "rude," and "unfriendly." The featured word is repeated in red type within a full-sentence definition. Crisp photographs show children of diverse backgrounds exhibiting each behavior. A "curious" boy holds a magnifying glass. A "funny" boy wears a fake nose and mustache, while "A Bossy person tells other people what to do."
Grades Pre-K–2
Content Area Language Arts
Instructional Value Descriptive writing; grammar
Text Structure Single letter (expanded)

Title *Eating the Alphabet: Fruits & Vegetables from A to Z*
Author /Illustrator Lois Ehlert
Publishing Company/Date Harcourt, Inc./1989
ISBN# 978-0152244354
Summary This book begins with an enticing call for children to eat their way through the healthy fruits and vegetables displayed in these bold and glorious watercolors. Each letter is presented in both uppercase and lowercase, and the names for the many fruits and vegetables illustrated for each letter are also repeated in both uppercase and lowercase. A useful glossary includes for each entry a thumbnail picture, a pronunciation guide, and a description, including how the food is grown and what it tastes like.
Grades Pre-K–2
Content Area Language Arts and Science
Instructional Value Vocabulary; life science
Text Structure Single letter

Title *G Is for Gold Medal*
Author Brad Herzog
Illustrator Doug Bowles
Publishing Company/Date Sleeping Bear Press/2011
ISBN# 978-1585364626
Summary Here the alphabet serves as a jumping-off point for sharing loads of interesting facts about Olympic events and famous Olympians, as well as a four-lined poem for each letter. From the first Olympics in Greece to our modern-day extravaganza, the spirit of excellence and the inspirational stories can spark kids to do their own personal best. Colorful illustrations, from a TV camera perspective, offer optimal views of the action. Each letter is presented in both uppercase and lowercase. In the back of the book is a listing of the Summer and Winter Olympic sites and dates.
Grades 3–6
Content Area Language Arts and Social Studies
Instructional Value Rhyme and rhythm; history
Text Structure Conceptual text

Title *C Is for Curious: An ABC of Feelings*
Author/Illustrator Woodleigh Hubbard
Publishing Company/Date Chronicle Books/1990
ISBN# 978-0877016793
Summary A range of emotions from "Angry" to "Zealous" is explored and explained through bold, energetic acrylic illustrations. A restless cow chews on its tail; the shy cat hides behind the couch. Some animal figures are identifiable; others are more imaginative and, like the emotion, open to interpretation. There is a dreamlike quality that edges toward a more sophisticated expression of each emotion. Only the capitalized word of the emotion is presented, with its first letter in a contrasting color.
Grades Pre-K–2
Content Area Language Arts
Instructional Value Grammar
Text Structure Single letter

Title *A–Z of the World Cup*
Author Michael Hurley
Photographer Various
Publishing Company/Date Raintree/2014
ISBN# 978-1406266252
Summary This comprehensive tour through all things related to soccer associates each capital letter with several words beginning with that letter; for example, A is for "African Representation," "Argentina," and "Azteca Stadium"; R is for "Red Card" and "Russia." The history, teams, players, rules, and statistics of the World Cup are among the

topics covered. The photographs are of professional events and capture the energy of the game. Charts and maps are also presented to support the newspaper-like text focused on presenting the highlights in readable bites. Over a dozen words are presented in a glossary, and further references, Web sites, and an index are also given.

Grades 3–6 and 7–12
Content Area Social Studies
Instructional Value Culture; geography; history
Text Structure Conceptual text

Title *On Your Toes: A Ballet ABC*
Author/Illustrator Rachel Isadora
Publishing Company/Date Greenwillow Books/2003
ISBN# 978-0060502386
Summary This book showcases both the dedication to this dance form and its glamour. Colored pastel illustrations capture behind-the-scenes sights and close-ups for the chosen single words for each letter of the alphabet. There is a sense of magic and an excitement to perform. The diverse children depicted are all of early elementary-school age. Letters are shown in capital form and in a contrasting color above the associated word. A glossary gives further explanation for the words, including "arabesque," "en pointe," "makeup," "tutu," and "zipper."

Grades Pre-K–2
Content Area Language Arts
Instructional Value Vocabulary
Text Structure Single letter

Title *F Is for Feelings*
Author Goldie Millar and Lisa A. Berger
Illustrator Hazel Mitchell
Publishing Company/Date Free Spirit Publishing/2014
ISBN# 978-1575424767
Summary This book is designed to encourage children to develop a richer vocabulary and to be more effective in their conversations about their emotions. Feelings are separated into feeling good and not so good, rather than into "good" and "bad" feelings. Each letter of the alphabet is shown in capital form and associated with a "feeling" word. Below "A is afraid," and an illustration of a young boy on the first day of school, is a descriptive sentence: "I am scared." Subsequent pages follow this format and include focus words like "brave," "confused," "determined," "impatient," "quiet," "terrific," and "zany." The capital and lowercase letters are presented in an upper corner. A guide to how to use the book and follow-up activities for parents and teachers are in the back of the book.

Grades Pre-K–2
Content Area Language Arts

Instructional Value Grammar
Text Structure Single letter (expanded)

Title *Alphabet Fun: Making Letters with Your Body*
Author/Illustrator Isobel Thomas
Publishing Company/Date Heinemann/2014
ISBN# 978-1432988029
Summary Young children are the stars in this alphabet book focused on the shapes of the letters. On each page children are photographed in varying poses to fill in the outline of each capital and lowercase letter. For the capital letter A, two similar-sized brown-haired boys wearing matching blue shirts link arms and lean toward each other. One of the boys then curls up to fit into the pale blue outline of the lowercase letter A. Subsequent pages show a diverse group of kids participating in this active alphabetic creation. The letters in both capital and lowercase are repeated next to the photographs. A list of activities focused on literacy learning and physical development is in the back of the book.
Grades Pre-K–2
Content Area Fine Arts
Instructional Value Observation and perception
Text Structure Single letter

History

Title *P Is for Pirate: A Pirate Alphabet*
Author Eve Bunting
Illustrator John Manders
Publishing Company/Date Sleeping Bear Press/2014
ISBN# 978-1585368150
Summary A host of cartoon pirates with exaggerated grins, eager for adventure, take readers on an alphabetical tour of a pirate's life. Each capital letter is paired with a focus word, which is then the subject of a four-line poem. A side panel offers more narrative detail. Focus words include "cutlass," "flogging," and "gold," as well as many famous pirates, such as Black Bart, William Kidd, Grace O'Malley, and Edward Teach (Blackbeard). The watercolor illustrations capture the grit and romance of a pirate's life.
Grades 3–6
Content Area Language Arts and Social Studies
Instructional Value Rhyme and rhythm; history
Text Structure Conceptual text

Title *America: A Patriotic Primer*
Author Lynne Cheney
Illustrator Robin Preiss Glasser

Publishing Company/Date Simon & Schuster Books for Young Readers/2002
ISBN# 978-0689851926
Summary Each capital letter is associated with an event, a concept, or a person that exemplifies the American heritage and spirit. America, declaration, freedom, ideals, Madison, suffrage, and Washington are among the topics covered. A one- or two-sentence text elaborates, but it is the tiny, detailed illustrations completely filling each page that give so much spark and color to this book. One spread has a map of the United States with several tiny drawings of monuments or resources. A frame around the page includes dozens more drawings of holidays celebrated in the United States.
Grades 3–6
Content Area Social Studies
Instructional Value History
Text Structure Single letter (expanded)

Title *Amelia to Zora: Twenty-Six Women Who Changed the World*
Author Cynthia Chin-Lee
Illustrator Megan Halsey and Sean Addy
Publishing Company/Date Charlesbridge/2005
ISBN# 978-1570915222
Summary Twenty-six amazing women are highlighted in this inspiring and encouraging text. Each capital letter is associated with the name of a famous 20th-century woman whose history, trials, contributions, and legacy are explained in a three-paragraph narrative and motivational quote. The mixed-media collage illustrations show each woman with key attributes or associations; Amelia Earhart is shown wearing her flying cap, and Rachel Carson is shown with birds perched on her shoulders. Astronomers, athletes, architects, journalists, and diplomats are among the women highlighted. The bibliography offers opportunities for further research.
Grades 3–6
Content Area Social Studies
Instructional Value History
Text Structure Conceptual text

Title *D Is for Drums: A Colonial Williamsburg ABC*
Author/Illustrator Kay Chorao
Publishing Company/Date Harry N. Abrams, Inc./2004
ISBN# 978-0810949270
Summary This book is a charming and detailed presentation of American colonial daily life. Maps of historic Williamsburg are endpapers, and hand-drawn figures twist and link hands to form each letter in the manner of period primers. A larger, capital version of each letter fills the page and is surrounded by numerous objects from colonial life. The vocabulary and detailed drawings will delight a budding historian, and the soft palette

of the drawings is enchanting. "Apothecary," "churn," "ewe," "necessary," and "riding chairs" are among the words featured.

Grades 3–6

Content Area Language Arts and Social Studies

Instructional Value Vocabulary; history

Text Structure Single letter (expanded)

Title *O Is for Old Dominion: A Virginia Alphabet*

Author Pamela Duncan Edwards

Illustrator Troy Howell

Publishing Company/Date Sleeping Bear Press/2005

ISBN# 978-1-585361618

Summary The state of Virginia is featured in this richly illustrated book. Both the history and the present-day attractions of the state are topics for each of the letters, which are presented in both capital and lowercase form. For the younger child, simple rhymes capture the theme, and on side panels the older child will discover the fascinating facts that put the historical figure or event into context. Fifteen questions on a back spread offer a test for the careful reader. Answers, printed upside down, are given as well. This book is part of an outstanding 51-book series entitled *Discover America State by State,* published by Sleeping Bear Press.

Grades 3–6

Content Area Language Arts and Social Studies

Instructional Value Rhyme and rhythm; culture; geography; history

Text Structure Conceptual text

Title *D Is for Democracy: A Citizen's Alphabet*

Author Elissa Grodin

Illustrator Victor Juhasz

Publishing Company/Date Sleeping Bear Press/2004

ISBN# 978-1585362349

Summary This engaging and thought-provoking book presents the development of U.S. government structure as well as democratic concepts and fascinating historical figures (like immigration and Dr. Martin Luther King Jr.). The letters are presented in both uppercase and lowercase and appear again at the start of a lyrical four-line poem. Covering topics from amendments, Congress, elections, the judicial branch, and political parties to religious freedom, each is supported with a compelling narrative rich with detail and vocabulary. The colored pencil and watercolor illustrations capture the energy and expressions of the people as well as the symbolism of these events. A spread in the back of the book suggests ways that young people can be involved in democracy (like staying informed, discussing an issue, and attending a city council meeting).

Grades 3–6
Content Area Language Arts and Social Studies
Instructional Value Rhyme and rhythm; history
Text Structure Conceptual Text

Title *Yankee Doodle America: The Spirit of 1776 from A to Z*
Author/Illustrator Wendell Minor
Publishing Company/Date G. P. Putnam's Sons/2006
ISBN# 978-0399240034
Summary Fans of American history from 1765 to 1783 will delight in this invitation to take a historical journey on horseback or by stagecoach, noticing the hand-painted wooden signs of inns and taverns along the way. Each letter of the alphabet is in capital form and is associated with a historical reference, such as "Yorktown," or with a concept like "independence" and "liberty." The five- or six-sentence descriptions are concise and inspiring. A timeline of important dates is also provided, bringing together the entire story.
Grades 3–6
Content Area Social Studies
Instructional Value History
Text Structure Single letter (expanded)

Title *Walden Then & Now: An Alphabetical Tour of Henry Thoreau's Pond*
Author/Illustrator Michael McCurdy
Publishing Company/Date Charlesbridge/2010
ISBN# 978-1580892537
Summary This book is a tribute to this influential figure in American history and captures the natural beauty of Walden Pond. The journey around the pond includes the animals, crops, seasons, and emotions found there. A simple rhyme for each capital letter of the alphabet is supported by text that weaves together the past and present of Walden Pond. The woodcut black-and-white illustrations underscore the simplicity and rich texture of life on Walden Pond. A spread in the back of the book details where references to the words chosen for the alphabet are to be found in Thoreau's writings.
Grades 7–12
Content Area Language Arts
Instructional Value Descriptive writing
Text Structure Conceptual text

Title *A Is for Abraham: A Jewish Family Alphabet*
Author Richard Michelson
Illustrator Ron Mazellan
Publishing Company/Date Sleeping Bear Press/2008

ISBN# 978-1585363223

Summary Luminous illustrations superbly weave together the past and the present, creating a compelling look at Jewish culture. The letters are presented in uppercase and lowercase and again at the start of a four-line poem about the featured word. Additional narrative along a side column provides a basic context for the multidimensional subjects, which include famous people like Abraham, David, and Queen Esther and traditions and places like bar and bat mitzvahs, the Torah, Jerusalem, and Passover. A Hebrew alphabet appears in the back of the book.

Grades 3–6

Content Area Language Arts and Social Studies

Instructional Value Rhyme and rhythm; culture; history

Text Structure Conceptual text

Title *B Is for Bookworm: A Library Alphabet*

Author Anita C. Prieto

Illustrator Renée Graef

Publishing Company/Date Sleeping Bear Press/2005

ISBN# 978-1585361458

Summary The opportunities for discovery, as well as historical events, are the focus of this sweeping treatment of the subject of libraries. From "author," "bookworm," "Dewey," and "Gutenberg" to "illustration," "knowing," "Library of Congress," and "quest," each focus word is the topic of a four-line poem and then covered in more detail in a narrative on a side panel. The letters are presented in capital form. Pastel illustrations show a diverse group of happy children and adults interacting. Additional fun facts about authors, books, and libraries are in the back.

Grades 3–6

Content Area Language Arts and Social Studies

Instructional Value Rhyme and rhythm; history

Text Structure Conceptual text

Title *Alphabetical: How Every Letter Tells a Story*

Author Michael Rosen

Publishing Company/Date Counterpoint/2015

ISBN# 978-1619024830

Summary In this engaging, 500-page academic work, each of the 26 chapters covers in vivid detail the history and pronunciation of each letter, as well as linking it to a topic: "A is for Alphabet," "B is for Battledore," and "C is for Ciphers." The letters are presented in uppercase, in a variety of stylized forms. The narrative is filled with fascinating facts covering a vast range of topics from Beowulf to rappers. An "Oulipo Olympics" section suggesting 20 clever alphabet games further inspires a love of language. An extensive listing of additional references and a comprehensive index are also provided.

Grades 7–12
Content Area Language Arts
Instructional Value Descriptive writing
Text Structure Conceptual text

Title *D Is for Drinking Gourd: An African American Alphabet*
Author Nancy I. Sanders
Illustrator E. B. Lewis
Publishing Company/Date Sleeping Bear Press/2007
ISBN# 978-1585362936
Summary This inspiring book shares a wealth of history about remarkable African Americans and their achievements. The letters are presented in both uppercase and lowercase and appear again at the start of a lyrical four-line poem. Topics including abolitionists, buffalo soldiers, emancipation, Harlem, Malcolm X, and Zion are each supported with several paragraphs of compelling narrative, rich with detail and vocabulary. The watercolor illustrations capture the expressions, strength, and beauty of the people and the powerful symbolism of these events.
Grades 3–6
Content Area Language Arts and Social Studies
Instructional Value Rhyme and rhythm; history
Text Structure Conceptual text

Title *Appleseed to Zamboni: Famous Men from A to Z*
Author/Illustrator Mary Elizabeth Salzmann
Publishing Company/Date ABDO Publishing Company/2008
ISBN# 978-1604530124
Summary The last names of 26 famous men are the focus for this alphabetic tour. Inventors, diplomats, scientists, entertainment figures, and leaders are included. The names include Johnny Appleseed, Walt Disney, Galileo Galilei, and Malcolm X. A two-sentence summary of their contribution is next to a photograph or other artistic likeness, and a "Guess what?" feature expands the reading experience, offering additional information. The letters are presented in capital and lowercase form. A two-page glossary explains important terms, and there is another listing of over 50 famous men.
Grades 3–6
Content Area Social Studies
Instructional Value History
Text Structure Conceptual Text

Title *Rad American Women A–Z: Rebels, Trailblazers, and Visionaries Who Shaped Our History . . . and Our Future!*
Author Kate Schatz

Illustrator Miriam Klein Stahl

Publishing Company/Date City Lights Books/2015

ISBN# 978-0872866836

Summary This rousing tribute to history-making women, from activist Angela Davis to novelist Zora Neale Hurston, offers powerful narratives that are sure to inspire. A profile is paired with each capital letter of the alphabet. The bold black-and-white paper cutout image of each woman is set against a strong, vivid color, lending to the energy and power this book packs. An alphabetical listing, with definitions, of 26 things a reader can do to be rad is in the back of the book, beginning with "act," "believe," "create," and "dare." A listing of other books and Web sites about rad women is also in the back of the book.

Grades 7–12

Content Area Social Studies

Instructional Value History

Text Structure Conceptual text

Title *Abe Lincoln: His Wit and Wisdom from A–Z*

Author Alan Schroeder

Illustrator John O'Brien

Publishing Company/Date Holiday House/2015

ISBN# 978-0823424207

Summary Brimming with anecdotal facts and covering major events of historical importance too, this journey through the alphabet also brings humor and quirkiness to this American icon. Emphasizing both his leadership and his humble beginnings, each letter is presented in capital form and is associated with a word that becomes the topic for many facts and anecdotes that humanize this great American figure. The drawings are humorous; Abe Lincoln clears land as a child, and the trees stack into a canister of Lincoln Logs.

Grades 3–6 and 7–12

Content Area Social Studies

Instructional Value History

Text Structure Conceptual text

Title *Ben Franklin: His Wit and Wisdom from A–Z*

Author Alan Schroeder

Illustrator John O'Brien

Publishing Company/Date Holiday House/2011

ISBN# 978-0823419500

Summary The many accomplishments, talents, and facets of Benjamin Franklin offer a wealth of material for this tour of the alphabet. Each letter, presented in capital form, is associated with a word that prompts an interesting fact. Additional words beginning with the featured letter are offered as well, with a short sentence or two of explanation.

The humorous, energetic, and detailed drawings add to the feel of inventiveness, surprise, and amusement.

Grades 3–6 and 7–12

Content Area Social Studies

Instructional Value History

Text Structure Conceptual text

Title *T Is for* Titanic

Author Debbie and Michael Shoulders

Illustrator Gijsbert van Frankenhuyzen

Publishing Company/Date Sleeping Bear Press/2011

ISBN# 978-1585361762

Summary Interesting facts and poignant stories about the fateful voyage of RMS *Titanic* and its eclectic group of 2,000 passengers include those of the captain; first-, second-, and third-class passengers; and even dogs. Parts of the ship, like the bridge and lifeboats, as well as recent inventions of the time (the Kodak camera), are discussed with several paragraphs of compelling narrative. The letters are presented in both uppercase and lowercase and appear again at the start of a lyrical four-line poem. The illustrations capture the styles of that era and this engineering marvel.

Grades 3–6

Content Area Language Arts and Social Studies

Instructional Value Rhyme and rhythm; history

Text Structure Conceptual text

Title *N Is for Our Nation's Capital: A Washington DC Alphabet*

Author Marie and Roland Smith

Illustrator Barbara Leonard Gibson

Publishing Company/Date Sleeping Bear Press/2005

ISBN# 978-1585361489

Summary This tribute to the nation's capital showcases its history and beauty through engaging rhymes for young readers paired with more detailed text for older readers. Supporting the text are beautiful watercolors that are like tourist snapshots of monuments or action shots of historical moments. The city is shown as a living, breathing place. Questions and answers are at the back of the book for the reader who wants further challenge. This book is part of an outstanding series entitled *Discover America State by State,* published by Sleeping Bear Press.

Grades 3–6

Content Area Language Arts and Social Studies

Instructional Value Rhyme and rhythm; history

Text Structure Conceptual text

Title *T Is for Time*
Author Marie and Roland Smith
Illustrator Renée Graef
Publishing Company/Date Sleeping Bear Press/2015
ISBN# 978-1585365128
Summary From the earliest understanding of the passage of time to our current understanding of the solar system, the importance of the concept of time is emphasized. Next to each capital and lowercase letter is a four-line poem that introduces the focus word. A more detailed explanatory text is presented on a side panel. A wealth of information about time is shared, from concepts such as daylight savings time and units, to inventors like Einstein and Harrison. The pastel and pencil illustrations offer numerous details, giving the book a nostalgic quality, yet still allowing it to inspire budding scientists.
Grades 7–12
Content Area Language Arts and Social Studies
Instructional Value Rhyme and rhythm; history
Text Structure Conceptual text

Title *A Apple Pie*
Author/Illustrator Gennady Spirin
Publishing Company/Date Philomel Books/2005
ISBN# 978-0399239816
Summary In exquisite detail, the illustrations bring to life a charming 17th-century English alphabet rhyme that chronicles the longing for and ultimate enjoyment of an apple pie: "A apple pie, B bit it, C cut it, D dealt it." Each letter is presented in several ways: as a large frame into which the illustration is set; as a capital and lowercase letter both printed and in cursive; and, yet again, within a phrase. Sweet, tiny animal figures with names beginning with the featured letter appear in a lower corner. The careful details of the wildflowers, the butterflies, and the children's period clothing show a richness in color and texture and are as scrumptious visually as the pie itself.
Grades All ages
Content Area Social Studies
Instructional Value History
Text Structure Single letter

Title *I Is for Idea*
Author Marcia Schonberg
Illustrator Kandy Radzinski
Publishing Company/Date Sleeping Bear Press/2005
ISBN# 978-1585362578

Summary This book celebrates human ingenuity and many inventions key to our modern life, from materials such as aluminum, Kevlar, and rubber to conveniences such as elevators, frozen foods, and microwaves. A four-line poem accompanies each finely drawn, detailed illustration, and a side panel offers further information, including how the item was invented and by whom, as well as lots of fun trivia for the curious mind. An appendix of 14 questions with answers, ("What invention made blue jeans popular in the US? Answer: copper rivets") adds further dimension to this topic.
Grades 3–6
Content Area Language Arts and Social Studies
Instructional Value Rhyme and rhythm; history
Text Structure Conceptual text

Title *A Is for America: A Patriotic Alphabet Book*
Author Tanya Lee Stone
Illustrator Gerald Kelley
Publishing Company/Date Price Stern Sloan/2011
ISBN# 978-0843198775
Summary Readers are invited to watch an elementary school play where famous Americans, events, and symbols are proudly portrayed. The colorful, cartoon-style illustrations show bright-faced students and an occasional adult filling in the roles. The illustrations clearly spell out the characters (e.g., each Supreme Court justice holds an oversized gavel bearing the justice's name). Each capital letter, which is associated with a word, is followed by a rhyming three-line text. For "President" the text reads, "Each term we get to choose/Who will run our country/And listen to our views."
Grades 3–6
Content Area Social Studies
Instructional Value History
Text Structure Conceptual text

Title *B Is for Beacon: A Great Lakes Lighthouse Alphabet*
Author Helen L. Wilbur
Illustrator Renée Graf
Publishing Company/Date Sleeping Bear Press/2016
ISBN# 978-1585369164
Summary The vast network of rivers and canals that connect the Great Lakes is an active waterway. Lighthouses have helped protect travelers for hundreds of years. Their symbolism of loyalty and courage is explored through short poems, each beginning with a capital letter. An explanatory text in a side panel further details their history. The black-outlined illustrations play on the remote beauty of these lighthouses. Focus words include "beacon," "jetty," "lens," "rescue," and "yesterday."
Grades 3–6

Content Area Language Arts and Social Studies
Instructional Value Rhyme and rhythm; culture; geography; history
Text Structure Conceptual text

Holidays

Title *ABC Hanukkah Hunt*
Author Tilda Balsley
Illustrator Helen Poole
Publishing Company/Date Kar-Ben Publishing/2013
ISBN# 978-1467704205
Summary The eight-day Festival of Lights is explained through the foods, gifts, and symbols of Hanukkah. The rhyming text begins with some history and then focuses on the celebration. The text often contains a question, prompting readers to point to an object: "King Antiochus! Where is he? He would not let the Jews be free" or "Which Menorah shows day three? Count the flames and you will see." The digital cartoons depict warm, friendly faces and the enjoyment of family time and traditions. The featured letter of the alphabet is capitalized within the sentence. Also note Tilda Balsley's *ABC Passover Hunt* (2016).
Grades Pre-K–2
Content Area Social Studies
Instructional Value Culture; history
Text Structure Single letter (expanded)

Title *Mary Engelbreit's A Merry Little Christmas: Celebrate from A to Z*
Author/Illustrator Mary Engelbreit
Publishing Company/Date HarperCollins/2006
ISBN# 978-0060741587
Summary Adorable animals play in the snow, make a gingerbread cottage, decorate the Christmas tree, and eagerly wait for Santa. Each cheery, detailed illustration is done with pen-and-ink outline and colorful marker and colored pencil and expresses the magic and charm of Christmastime and the coziness of this happy village. The capital letters begin the one- or two-sentence text, such as "M is for mittens, wooly and snug. Mom helps put them on and then gives me a hug."
Grades Pre-K–2
Content Area Language Arts
Instructional Value Rhyme and rhythm
Text Structure Single letter (expanded)

Title *ABC's of Easter*
Author/Illustrator Patricia Reeder Eubank
Publishing Company/Date Ideals Children's Books/2010

ISBN# 978-0824956172

Summary In these colorful and sweetly detailed illustrations, three little rabbits interact with a myriad of Easter-related items, from baskets of flowers to tiny baby animals to candies. Every letter is presented in uppercase form on a brightly colored egg. The letter is used again in a largely alliterative listing of Easter-related items. Finding the rabbits on each page will be engaging for the very young. Also note Eubank's *Valentine ABCs* (2008*) and ABC's of Halloween* (2013).

Grades Pre-K–2

Content Area Language Arts

Instructional Value Alliteration; phonemic awareness; vocabulary

Text Structure Single letter (expanded)

Title *Alpha Oops! H Is for Halloween*

Author Alethea Kontis

Illustrator Bob Kolar

Publishing Company/Date Candlewick Press/2010

ISBN# 978-0763639662

Summary The letter Z directs a play with a cast of alphabet actors including P (for "pirate"), G (for "goblin"), and V (for "vampire"). The bold capital letters appear in random order as actors in the play with tiny arms, legs, eyes, and mouths. Along the bottom of the page, the letters of the alphabet that appear in the story above are presented on pumpkins that assemble themselves in correct order with each successive page. The vivid color and the excitement of Halloween costumes add to the element of mayhem.

Grades Pre-K–2

Content Area Language Arts

Instructional Value Alphabetic principle

Text Structure Hidden letter

Title *B Is for Bethlehem: A Christmas Alphabet*

Author Isabel Wilner

Illustrator Elisa Kleven

Publishing Company/Date Ideals Children's Books/2015

ISBN# 978-0824956745

Summary Mixed-media collages of painting and cut paper create charming folk-art styled images that share the story of Jesus's birth, from the decree of Emperor Augustus to the Three Wise Men. Many of the figures include children dancing and singing in celebration. Each capital letter begins a couplet. For W, the text reads, "W's for Worship. O come and adore. In starlight, in candlelight, glad carols soar."

Grades Pre-K–2

Content Area Language Arts

Instructional Value Rhyme and rhythm

Text Structure Single letter (expanded)

Mathematics

Title *123 versus ABC*
Author/Illustrator Mike Boldt
Publishing Company/Date Harper/2013
ISBN# 978-0062102997
Summary An animated book where the numbers and letters each want to be the star of the story. Beginning with one alligator and moving on to two bears arriving in three cars, the book continues listing common objects or animals and pairing them with the next successive number. The playful, expressive illustrations become ever more crowded, offering readers counting opportunities. The letters are presented in capital form at the beginning of the focus word.
Grades Pre-K–2
Content Area Language Arts and Mathematics
Instructional Value Number and operation
Text Structure Single letter

Title *Poor Puppy and Bad Kitty*
Author/Illustrator Nick Bruel
Publishing Company/Date Roaring Book Press/2012
ISBN# 978-1596438446
Summary Kitty doesn't want to play with Puppy, so Puppy plays with an alphabetical assortment of things, each of which is further associated with a number: "1 Airplane," "2 Balls," "3 Cars," "4 Dolls," etc. Then Puppy takes a nap and dreams of a worldwide alphabetical journey with Kitty ("apple bobbing in Antarctica," "baseball in Brazil," "checkers in Canada"). Each time the featured letter appears in the text, it is red and capitalized. The page is divided so that several letters are presented on a spread. The illustrations are energetic and colorful and showcase the playful spirit of the puppy.
Grades Pre-K–2
Content Area Language Arts and Mathematics
Instructional Value Alliteration; number and operation
Text Structure Single letter (expanded)

Title *8: An Animal Alphabet*
Author/Illustrator Elisha Cooper
Publishing Company/Date Orchard Books/2015
ISBN# 978-0545470834
Summary Each page contains a capital and a lowercase letter, along with watercolors of numerous animals whose names start with that letter. One of the animals is depicted eight times, so the reader is encouraged to count. The list of animals depicted, sometimes as many as a dozen, is along the bottom edge and include names of some less familiar animals. The animals are not shown to scale, but rather they appear much like loose

puzzle pieces, evenly scattered about the page. The illustrations are detailed enough to convey the important characteristics of each animal. A "Did you know?" glossary at the end of the book shares a thumbnail illustration of each of the 184 animals found in the book, with its name and a unique characteristic or some trivia about each animal.

Grades Pre-K–2

Content Area Mathematics and Science

Instructional Value Number and operations; life science

Text Structure Single letter (expanded)

Title *Angles to Zeros: Mathematics from A to Z*

Author/Illustrator Colleen Dolphin

Publishing Company/Date ABDO/2008

ISBN# 978-1604530117

Summary Each of the twenty-six letters is presented with one or two mathematical terms. Some of the terms are "addition," "angle," "billion," "estimate," "even number," "quotient," "volume," and "Y-axis." Each term is clearly defined with a few simple sentences. Photographs of children or common objects help to round out the explanation. A "Guess what?" feature expands the reading experience, offering additional information. The letters are presented in capital and lowercase form. A two-page glossary explains important terms, and another page lists over 50 additional mathematics terms.

Grades 3–6

Content Area Mathematics

Instructional Value Geometry; measurement; number and operation

Text Structure Conceptual text

Title *26 Letters and 99 Cents*

Author/Photographer Tanya Hoban

Publishing Company/Date Turtleback/1995

ISBN# 978-0613001908

Summary Crisp photographs of bright, colorful plastic uppercase and lowercase letters are paired with an object beginning with that letter. "Aa" is paired with a toy airplane; "Bb" is paired with a bicycle. The objects are commonplace and expected (a xylophone, a yoyo, and a zipper for X, Y, and Z). When the book is turned over and read again, the cardinal numbers 1–99 are paired with the equivalent amount in coins.

Grades Pre-K–2

Content Area Mathematics

Instructional Value Number and operations

Text Structure Single letter

Title *Alphabet Explosion! Search and Count from Alien to Zebra*

Author/Illustrator John Nickle

Publishing Company/Date Schwartz & Wade Books/2006

ISBN# 978-0375935985

Summary In this seek-and-find alphabet book, each letter appears on a page with a number, indicating the number of times it can be found within an illustration (e.g., "22 A's"). The letters also appear additional times within the colorful, surreal, and dreamlike illustrations composed of animals, objects, and actions suspended in a sea of color. The author introduces the book with the rules of the challenging game. An answer key with a full list of items is in the back of the book and includes words such as "aiming," "honeycomb," "narwhal," and "violets."

Grades 3–6

Content Area Language Arts and Mathematics

Instructional Value Vocabulary; number and operations

Text Structure Hidden letter

Title *G Is for Googol: A Math Alphabet Book*

Author David Schwartz

Illustrator Marissa Moss

Publishing Company/Date Tricycle Press/1998

ISBN# 978-1883672584

Summary An enormous range of topics is included in this factual yet approachable and even humorous text. Each capital letter is associated with a math word; for example, "A is for Abacus," "B is for Binary," "C is for Cubit," "F is for Fibonacci," and "R is for Rhombicosidodecahedron." The text is engaging and conversational and emphasizes the importance of these discoveries in present-day life. The bright cartoon illustrations offer witty and playful commentary.

Grades 7–12

Content Area Mathematics

Instructional Value Geometry; measurement; number and operation

Text Structure Conceptual text

Mixed-Up Alphabet

Title Z Is for Moose

Author Kelly Bingham

Illustrator Paul O. Zelinsky

Publishing Company/Date Greenwillow Books/2012

ISBN# 978-0060799847

Summary In this humorous storyline, an impatient moose creates mayhem and lots of headache for the zebra that is trying to direct an orderly presentation of the alphabet. After the first few letters, the moose pops up on stage, begging and sometimes stealing the spotlight. When the moose's actual turn is overlooked, it gets mad and creates even more chaos. Each letter is presented in uppercase and is associated with an object. The illustrations are colorful and show the emotions and funny antics of the moose and zebra, whose friendship is preserved in the end.

Grades Pre-K–2

Content Area Language Arts

Instructional Value Descriptive writing

Text Structure Single letter (expanded)

Title *Q Is for Duck: An Alphabet Guessing Game*

Author Mary Elting and Michael Folsom

Illustrator Jack Kent

Publishing Company/Date Perfection Learning/2005

ISBN# 978-0756978716

Summary Every letter of the alphabet is first shown in a colorful, large capital form and then associated with a word that does not begin with the featured letter. Here begins the riddle that is answered on the succeeding page. "A is for Zoo. Why?" (Turn the page.) "Because Animals live in Zoos." The featured letter is also capitalized in a contrasting color within the associated word. There is rhythm to this riddle book, and the association of each animal with the sound it makes is engaging. The illustrations are humorous and lend a sense of silliness and fun.

Grades Pre-K–2

Content Area Language Arts

Instructional Value Descriptive writing

Text Structure Hidden letter

Title *The Cow Is Mooing Anyhow: A Scrambled Alphabet Book to Be Read at Breakfast*

Author Laura Geringer

Illustrator Dirk Zimmer

Publishing Company/Date Harper Trophy/1991

ISBN# 978-0060219864

Summary A young girl's breakfast is continuously interrupted by an assortment of animals. The twist is that the alphabet animals appear in random order. First comes the letter I with "the Iguanas, the iguanas come in their pajamas." The detailed illustrations show nervous energy in the line work supporting the chaos of the morning clutter lying about, which only gets more jumbled with each new animal's appearance. Letters introduced on the previous spread appear in capital form within the white frame surrounding the image. The completed alphabet is shown on a final spread, as well as drawings of each animal with its associated letter in capital form and the name of the animal.

Grades Pre-K–2

Content Area Language Arts

Instructional Value Alphabetic principle; vocabulary

Text Structure Hidden letter

Title *AlphaOops! The Day Z Went First*
Author Alethea Kontis
Illustrator Bob Kolar
Publishing Company/Date Candlewick Press/2006
ISBN# 978-0763627287
Summary In this antics-filled book, the letter Z convinces all of the other letters to run the alphabet show backwards. Then the letter P has its own ideas, and again the alphabet goes topsy-turvy. The capital letters star as themselves, holding or wearing the item they are associated with. The Y is knitting with yarn, and the B holds a balloon. Children will enjoy the snappy dialogue and keeping track of the correct order of the alphabet.
Grades Pre-K–2
Content Area Language Arts
Instructional Value Alphabetic principle
Text Structure Hidden letter

Title *Chicka Chicka Boom Boom*
Author Bill Martin Jr. and John Archambault
Illustrator Lois Ehlert
Publishing Company/Date Simon & Schuster Books for Young Readers/1989
ISBN# 978-0671679491
Summary In this charming tale, bold, colorful letters race in alphabetical order up a coconut tree, which grows heavier and bends farther over with each addition. Young children will delight in the catchy rhymes and the suspense of wondering if there will be enough room in the tree for all of the letters. The chorus of "Chicka chicka boom boom!" will be fun to repeat over and over. The letters are tilted and animated further, especially after they all fall in a pile under the tree and recover again one by one, sporting Band-Aids or skinned knees. The text presents the alphabet in capital letters, while the illustrations show them as lowercase. Brightly colored polka-dot borders and the simple image of the coconut tree lend to the cheery and fun tropical atmosphere.
Grades Pre-K–2
Content Area Language Arts
Instructional Value Rhyme and rhythm
Text Structure Single letter (expanded)

Title *The Alphabet from Z to A (With Much Confusion on the Way)*
Author Judith Viorst
Illustrator Richard Hull
Publishing Company/Date Atheneum/1994
ISBN# 978-0689317682
Summary Moving backwards through the alphabet, this book shares some of the quirkiness and inconsistencies in the English language, like "Y is for Yew and You" and "V is for Vane, Vain and Vein." In the back of the book, there is a complete listing of all of the

objects to be found for each letter. The capital letters are presented within illustrations similar in style to medieval illuminated manuscripts. The intertwining objects allow the letter to become part of the ornamental and often surreal detail. These intricate, gem-like drawings cleverly combine each alphabetical list of objects.

Grades 3–6
Content Area Language Arts
Instructional Value Phonemic awareness
Text Structure Hidden letter

Title *Alphabet Mystery*
Author Audrey Wood
Illustrator Bruce Wood
Publishing Company/Date The Blue Sky Press/2003
ISBN# 978-0439443371
Summary The book begins with each lowercase letter in its own bunk bed, calling out its name in the final roll call of the day; but on this day, the X is missing. The storyline is engaging and invites the reader to participate as the letters search and recall the letter order. All of the other letters are set into action on magic flying pencils to find their friend X and solve the mystery. As the letters are referred to in the story, readers will look for them in the vivid, photorealistic illustrations. In the end, the X is found on the birthday cake: it is the only letter that stands for kisses.

Grades Pre-K–2
Content Area Language Arts
Instructional Value Alphabetic principle
Text Structure Hidden letter

Multicultural

Title *A Is for Asia*
Author Cynthia Chin-Lee
Illustrator Yumi Heo
Publishing Company/Date Orchard Books/1997
ISBN# 978-0531330111
Summary In broad and understandable terms, the complexity of Asian culture is broken down by describing important traditions, symbols, animals, and food. The word chosen to represent each letter of the alphabet is then written again in an Asian language ("Asia," for A, is also written in Tibetan; "batik," for B, is also written in Indonesian; "camel," for C, is also written in Arabic). The vastness of the lands that constitute Asia is mirrored in the sweeping, panoramic pen-and-ink drawings that pay homage to traditional two-dimensional drawing styles and use yellow and gold tones throughout. Capital letters are presented at the beginning of the paragraphs.

Grades 3–6
Content Area Social Studies
Instructional Value Culture; history
Text Structure Conceptual text

Title *Costa Rica ABCs: A Book About the People and Places of Costa Rica*
Author Sharon Katz Cooper
Illustrator Allen Eitzen
Publishing Company/Date Picture Window Books/2007
ISBN# 978-1404822498
Summary This is a well-researched tribute to the rich culture and natural beauty found in Costa Rica. Each letter is presented in uppercase and lowercase. For less familiar words, like "B is for Bribri," a phonetic pronunciation is given as well as the definition or explanation, along with a "Fast Fact" for an even deeper level of understanding. The illustrations are clear, colorful, and appealing, from art to coffee to rain forest. Pages in the back of the book offer some country facts, a glossary, and a few words to learn in Spanish.
Grades 3–6
Content Area Social Studies
Instructional Value Culture
Text Structure Conceptual text

Title *Alcatraz to Zanzibar: Famous Places from A to Z*
Author Colleen Dolphin
Illustrator Various
Publishing Company/Date ABDO Publishing Company/2009
ISBN# 978-1604534924
Summary Crisp photographs showcase 26 amazing places around the world, including the Himalayas, Machu Picchu, and the Taj Mahal. Each place is associated with a letter of the alphabet that appears in both uppercase and lowercase. A brief description of two or three sentences is written under the name of the place, as well as a "Guess what?" fact (e.g., "People used more than 1,000 elephants to help build the Taj Mahal"). A two-page glossary covers additional words such as "causeway," "goods," "tomb," and "wildlife." An additional listing of over 60 places offers even more opportunities for discovery.
Grades 3–6
Content Area Social Studies
Instructional Value Geography
Text Structure Single letter (expanded)

Title *Jambo Means Hello: Swahili Alphabet Book*
Author Muriel Feelings
Illustrator Tom Feelings

Publishing Company/Date Turtleback Books/1992

ISBN# 978-0881035278

Summary This Caldecott-winning book introduces the reader to Swahili words and the beauty and rich culture of East Africa. From the *arusi* (wedding) to the *zeze* (stringed instrument), each word is integral to life. As there is no Q or X in Swahili, those letters are omitted. The double-page layout has the uppercase letter of the alphabet in the upper left corner, followed by a Swahili word beginning with that letter and its definition. A pronunciation is given, as well as a short paragraph of explanation. The black-and-white illustrations of animals, people, and landscapes are atmospheric and majestic.

Caldecott Honor Book

Grades 3–6

Content Area Social Studies

Instructional Value Culture

Text Structure Single letter (expanded)

Title *E Is for Ethiopia*

Author Ashenafi Gudeta

Photographer Betelhem Abate et al.

Publishing Company/Date Francis Lincoln Children's Books/2011

ISBN# 978-1845078256

Summary Vivid photographs provide clear and instructive examples of current culture in Ethiopia. The text offers information on how people live and what they wear and eat. Every letter in the alphabet is shown in both uppercase and lowercase and is associated with a word. Some of the words are known to English-speaking children, like "basket" or "house"; others are likely unfamiliar (*aheya* means "donkey," and *weha* means "water"). This is part of a growing series of currently 24 *World Alphabets* books published by the Quatro Group. Other titles include *I Is for India, R Is for Russia* and *T Is for Turkey*.

Grades 3–6

Content Area Social Studies

Instructional Value Culture

Text Structure Single letter (expanded)

Title *Turtle Island Alphabet: A Lexicon of Native American Symbols and Culture*

Author Gerald Hausman

Publishing Company/Date St. Martin's Press/1992

ISBN# 978-0312071035

Summary "Turtle Island" is a Native American term for the earth, and this book shares the stories, images, and symbols that are significant to Native American life. The alphabetical listing of featured words is presented in uppercase letters at the beginning of each entry. One hundred and fifty photographs and drawings further detail the range of alphabetic topics, including "arrow," "basket," "bead," "buffalo," and "corn." Language and memory play an important role in this text, which combines poetry and storytelling to pay tribute to the cultures and lands of the American Indians.

Grades 7–12

Content Area Social Studies and Science

Instructional Value Culture; geography; history; earth science; life science

Text Structure Conceptual text

Title *P Is for Passport: A World Alphabet*

Author David Scillian

Illustrator Various

Publishing Company/Date Sleeping Bear Press/2003

ISBN# 978-1585361571

Summary This world tour celebrates both our global diversity and our common experience, from the basics like bread (a buttery bun in Britain, a bagel for those in Brooklyn, and a baguette in Bordeaux) to the variety of currency, languages, and music. Other topics include animals, deserts, faith, and the wonders of the world. The letters are presented in both uppercase and lowercase and appear again at the start of a lyrical six-line poem. The colorful illustrations were created by a variety of artists.

Grades 3–6

Content Area Language Arts and Social Studies

Instructional Value Rhyme and rhythm; culture

Text Structure Conceptual text

Nature

Title *A Gardener's Alphabet*

Author/Illustrator Mary Azarian

Publishing Company/Date Houghton Mifflin Company/2000

ISBN# 978-0618033805

Summary Following a two-page introduction sharing the author's love of gardening, a full-page woodcut illustration, hand-tinted with strong, colorful watercolor, appears for each letter. A single word in capital letters appears within each woodcut. Many of the words may be familiar to young readers, while others, like "topiary" and "xeriscape," although illustrated, may need further explanation. The simplicity adds to an ordered and tidy feeling. The scenes are charming and share the joy of tending a garden and the beauty found within.

Grades Pre-K–2

Content Area Science

Instructional Value Life science

Text Structure Single letter

Title *M Is for Majestic: A National Parks Alphabet*
Author David Domeniconi
Illustrator Pam Carroll
Publishing Company/Date Sleeping Bear Press/2003
ISBN# 978-1585361380
Summary The astounding and varied beauty of the U.S. national parks, from Acadia along Maine's rugged coast to Olympic National Park in Washington State, is highlighted. The dramatic illustrations include animals, plant life, rivers, and mountains, and they are often presented as if viewing a scrapbook where photos or mementos are taped to the page. People are shown swimming, canoeing, or exploring. Next to each capital and lowercase letter is a four-line poem that introduces the focus word, like "Everglades," "Hawaiian Volcanoes," "Mesa Verde," and "Yellowstone." A more detailed explanatory text is presented within a side panel.
Grades 3–6
Content Area Language Arts and Science
Instructional Value Rhyme and rhythm; earth science; life science
Text Structure Conceptual text

Title *Stargazer's Alphabet: Night-Sky Wonders from A to Z*
Author John Farrell
Publishing Company/Date Boyd Mills Press/2007
ISBN# 978-1590784662
Summary Beautiful full-bleed photographs capture the brilliance, depth, and wonder of space. From "Andromeda" to "Zodiac," the celestial topics are strung together with lyrical verses ("A is for Andromeda, our neighbor galaxy. B is for the Big Dipper, that's an easy one to see"). The letter featured is in capital form and in a different color from the rest of the text. Short descriptive text provides an introductory explanation and interesting facts about the planets and constellations. A glossary includes terms such as "asterism," "black hole," "light-year," "nebula," and "planisphere."
Grades 3–6 and 7–12
Content Area Science
Instructional Value Earth science
Text Structure Conceptual text

Title *A Is for Anaconda: A Rainforest Alphabet*
Author Anthony D. Fredericks
Illustrator Laura Regan
Publishing Company/Date Sleeping Bear Press/2009
ISBN# 978-1585363179
Summary A colorful array of tropical flora and fauna is the topic of this ecologically and environmentally focused book. Each letter is presented in uppercase and lowercase and begins

a four-line poem about the focus word. A side panel offers additional intriguing facts. Topics include "anaconda," "Brazil," "canopy," "jaguars," "medicine," "vanilla," and "xylem." The illustrations capture the textures and colors of this diverse and rich environment.

Grades 3–6

Content Area Language Arts and Science

Instructional Value Rhyme and rhythm; life science

Text Structure Conceptual text

Title *S Is for Save the Planet: A How-to-Be Green Alphabet*

Author Brad Herzog

Illustrator Linda Holt Ayriss

Publishing Company/Date Sleeping Bear Press/2009

ISBN# 978-1585364282

Summary Conveying important conservation steps and raising awareness of environmental issues are the overall aims of this alphabet book. Topics include "appreciation" (Earth Day), "daily decision" (paper or plastic), and "newspapers" (recycle). The letters are presented in both uppercase and lowercase and appear again at the start of an eight-line, two-stanza poem. Detailed colored-pencil and watercolor illustrations show children involved in protecting the environment. A page of Web resources offers opportunities for further learning.

Grades 3–6

Content Area Language Arts and Science

Instructional Value Rhyme and rhythm; earth science; life science

Text Structure Conceptual text

Title *West Coast Wild: A Nature Alphabet*

Author Deborah Hodge

Illustrator Karen Reczuch

Publishing Company/Date Groundwood Books/2015

ISBN# 978-1554984404

Summary The vast and breathtakingly beautiful Pacific coast offers much majestic scenery to explore, from the ancient rain forest to the cool ocean and all of the animals and ecosystems within. A capital letter associated with the focus word begins each paragraph for that letter. The watercolor illustrations offer lush detail, and the vantage point is typically at eye level with the animals featured. The language is vivid, full of similes and careful descriptions. Some of the words featured are "Dungeness crabs," "huckleberries," "limpets," and "wolves."

Grades 3–6

Content Area Science

Instructional Value Life science

Text Structure Single letter (expanded)

Title *Alison's Zinnia*

Author/Illustrator Anita Lobel

Publishing Company/Date Turtleback/1996

ISBN# 978-0613004244

Summary In these lush and delicately drawn botanical illustrations, a flower is highlighted and becomes the central illustration for each letter. Each capital letter is in boldface at the bottom of the page and begins the simple sentence that follows the pattern girl-verb-flower, such as "Alison acquired an Amaryllis for Beryl." The linking of one letter to the next creates a rhythmic flow where the last letter and page is "Zena zeroed in on a Zinnia for Alison," bringing the text through the full alphabetic circle. A smaller, enchanting illustration below the flower shows the girl delivering, jarring, quilting, tending (etc.) the flower.

Grades Pre-K–2

Content Area Language Arts and Science

Instructional Value Alliteration; life science

Text Structure Single letter (expanded)

Title *A Is for Autumn*

Author/Photographer Robert Maas

Publishing Company/Date Henry Holt and Company/2011

ISBN# 978-0805090932

Summary The beauty and richness of autumn comes alive through vibrant photographs and crisp narrative. Whether a distant view of a field or a group of bicyclists or a more close-up view of apples and frost, the opportunities to visually and physically enjoy the season are celebrated. Each capital letter is bold and begins a complete sentence that explains the photograph.

Grades Pre-K–2

Content Area Science

Instructional Value Earth science; life science

Text Structure Single letter (expanded)

Title *Alphabatics*

Author/ Illustrator Suse MacDonald

Publishing Company/Date Simon & Schuster Books for Young Readers/1986

ISBN# 978-0027615203

Summary Boldly colored uppercase and lowercase letters appear at the top left of every page. Below, in a series of boxes, the letter is presented again in one box and then transforms from left to right through each successive box to become a clean, simple graphic image of the word that is then presented fully on the right-hand page. The capital E tips backward and transforms to become the elephant's foot; the lowercase N takes flight and becomes a nest. The word beginning with the letter featured is written too. Just like an acrobat, these letters perform. This imaginative book will encourage creative thinking.

Caldecott Honor Book
Grades Pre-K–2
Content Area Fine Arts and Language Arts
Instructional Value Observation and perception; alphabetic principle
Text Structure Single letter (expanded)

Title *The Flower Alphabet Book*
Author Jerry Pallotta
Illustrator Leslie Evans
Publishing Company/Date Charlesbridge Publishing/1989
ISBN# 978-0881064599
Summary A blooming display of 26 gorgeous flowers is illustrated at their peak, full of color and perfection. An accompanying paragraph for each shares interesting facts about how the flowers grow, how they are used, or even how they got their name. Surrounding each presentation of a flower is an illustrated frame composed of landscapes, tables set for tea or farm animals, and in the bottom center of each frame is the letter of the alphabet in both capital and lowercase form. An "Artist's Note" page includes even more facts about each flower, inspiring those who love trivia and encouraging future gardeners. There are many more alphabet books created by Jerry Pallotta, covering a wide range of topics.
Grades Pre-K–2
Content Area Science
Instructional Value Life science
Text Structure Conceptual text

Title *Wildflower ABC: An Alphabet of Potato Prints*
Author/Illustrator Diana Pomeroy
Publishing Company/Date Harcourt Brace & Company/1997
ISBN# 978-0152010416
Summary Masterfully executed potato prints, with finely textured elements and shadings of color, make each of the wildflower illustrations appear as if pressed between the pages. The letters are presented in both capital and lowercase form and stand next to a single name of a wildflower. Some of the names may be challenging to pronounce ("Elecampane," "Nasturtium," "Rudbeckia," and "Xerophyllum tenax"). Others are more straightforward ("Bluebonnet," "Firecracker," "Lily," and "Poppy"). A listing of all of the wildflowers, giving their scientific names and a few facts, is included, along with a bibliography.
Grades Pre-K–2
Content Area Science
Instructional Value Life science
Text Structure Single letter

Title *Spring: An Alphabet Acrostic*
Author Steven Schnur
Illustrator Leslie Evans
Publishing Company/Date Clarion Books/1999
ISBN# 978-0395822692
Summary The season of spring is truly celebrated with 26 beautiful acrostic poems evoking the joy of emerging new life, beginning with the letter for the month of April ("After days of/Pouring/Rain, the last/Ice and snow finally/Leave the earth") and ending with "Zenith" ("Zucchinis and/Eggplants are greening/Now that summer/Is finally here and/ The hot sun is/High overheard"). The featured letter is large and capitalized and begins the poem. Strong, colorful, linoleum-cut illustrations show intimate scenes of nature, people, and animals. Find other seasons by the same author and illustrator in this same format: *Autumn: An Alphabet Acrostic* (1997), *Summer: An Alphabet Acrostic* (2001), and *Winter: An Alphabet Acrostic* (2002).
Grades Pre-K–2
Content Area Language Arts
Instructional Value Descriptive writing
Text Structure Single letter (expanded)

Title *Alphabet of Earth*
Author Barbie Heit Schwaeber
Illustrator Sally Vitsky
Publishing Company/Date Soundprints/2011
ISBN# 978-1592499960
Summary Reviewed by the Smithsonian, this alphabet book showcases our beautiful planet while encouraging young readers to be environmentally conscious. Each letter is presented in both uppercase and lowercase and is repeated again in capital form within the text. A gently rhyming four-line poem explains each featured word, including "air," "blizzard," "continents," "marsh," "quartz," and "zephyr." The images are created from paper collage and are bright and colorful. A poster, glossary, and sing-along CD are also included.
Grades 3–6
Content Area Science
Instructional Value Earth science
Text Structure Single letter (expanded)

Title *Q Is for Quark: A Science Alphabet Book*
Author David M. Schwartz
Illustrator Kim Doner
Publishing Company/Date Tricycle Press/2001
ISBN# 978-1582460215

Summary This is an entertaining and approachable resource. Each letter is presented in capital form and is associated with a variety of complex scientific topics, from "atoms," "black holes," and "clones" to "universe," "vortex," and "wow!" The text is clear and engaging, sharing both ancient views of the topic and modern understanding; interesting facts give perspective to these larger concepts. The practicality and usefulness of this knowledge is made evident by the everyday examples. Detailed cartoon illustrations, labeled diagrams, and witty side commentary offer bursts of color next to the narrative.
Grades 7–12
Content Area Science
Instructional Value Chemistry; earth science; life science; physics
Text Structure Conceptual text

Title *Tomorrow's Alphabet*
Author George Shannon
Illustrator Donald Crews
Publishing Company/Date Greenwillow Books/1996
ISBN# 978-0688135041
Summary Predicting what will become of an object is the concept behind this alphabet book: "A is for seed—tomorrow's APPLE." Each spread shares both the initial object and the resulting object, offering at a glance the entire transformation. Other connections include "C is for milk—tomorrow's CHEESE" and "X is for bones—tomorrow's X-RAY." Each colorful, bold capital letter is in an upper left corner. The large watercolor illustrations highlight the true transformation by showing how the texture, color, or size has changed. There is a peaceful stillness in the images. Most of the subjects refer to plants, food, and crafts.
Grades Pre=K–2
Content Area Science
Instructional Value Chemistry; earth science; life science; physics
Text Structure Conceptual text

Objects

Title *All About Boats A to Z*
Authors David and Zora Aiken
Illustrator David Aiken
Publishing Company/Date Schiffer Publishing/2012
ISBN# 978-0764341847
Summary The family fun of boating and the many activities and skills even the youngest crew members can use to help along the journey are the subjects of this book. A four-line verse introduces a boating term, and the cartoon-like pen and watercolor illustrations

offer details that young boaters will appreciate. The letters are presented in both capital and lowercase form in an upper corner. Boating terms include "anchor," "compass," "ensign," "galley," "transom," and "yawl."

Grades Pre-K–2

Content Area Language Arts

Instructional Value Alphabetic principle; rhyme and rhythm

Text Structure Conceptual text

Title *Ellsworth's Extraordinary Electric Ears and Other Amazing Alphabet Anecdotes*

Author/Illustrator Valorie Fisher

Publishing Company/Date Atheneum Books for Young Readers/2003

ISBN# 978-0689850301

Summary Each carefully composed scene is made of tiny plastic figures, paper cutouts, and repurposed objects, all illustrating an imaginative and fanciful alliterative sentence. A colorful capital letter begins each sentence and the name of its main character. The book begins with "Alistair had an alarming appetite for acrobats," where an opened-mouth alligator waits below the acrobat walking on the tightrope above. Armadillos, ants, apples, and airplanes also appear in the scene. The scenes are photographed so that only the foreground is in focus, giving a sense that the scene is in motion. A listing of objects is provided in the back of the book.

Grades Pre-K–2

Content Area Language Arts

Instructional Value Alliteration; vocabulary

Text Structure Single letter

Title *A Fabulous Fair Alphabet*

Author/Illustrator Debra Frasier

Publishing Company/Date Beach Lane Books/2010

ISBN# 978-1416998174

Summary This neon and candy-colored extravaganza of letters is pieced together from photographs of signs at state fairs and carnivals. Each page presents the uppercase letter in dozens of attention-grabbing styles. The target word or phrase ("arena," "barn," "dill pickle," "tractor," "unbelievable") is composed of letters from a variety of signs. A basic linear framework creates a minimalist notion of the target word, and then the letters fill in all of the gaps. The energy and buzz is electric, and the joy of a day at the fair is a strong theme throughout.

Grades Pre-K–2

Content Area Fine Arts and Language Arts

Instructional Value Graphic design; observation and perception; alphabetic principle

Text Structure Hidden letter

Title *ABC: A Child's First Alphabet Book*
Author/Illustrator Alison Jay
Publishing Company/Date Dutton Children's Books/2003
ISBN# 978-0525469513
Summary Each page illustrates an imaginative scene containing one large object and then several smaller objects whose names begin with a particular letter of the alphabet. Both capital and lowercase letters are presented along with a simple sentence in the "A is for Apple" format. The illustrations are in a folk art style, and the animals and humans with their elongated bodies interact in a dreamlike fashion. A subtle storyline is interwoven between the pages, so that in the end, all of the animals and people are united. A listing of all of the objects presented on each page is given at the end of the book.
Grades Pre-K–2
Content Area Language Arts
Instructional Value Alphabetic principle
Text Structure Single letter

Title *What Pete Ate from A–Z (Really!)*
Author/Illustrator Maira Kalman
Publishing Company/Date G. P. Putnam's Sons/2001
ISBN# 978-0399233623
Summary Poppy's dog Pete has an insatiable appetite and doesn't seem to mind eating things that most would find inedible, making him a nuisance to everyone. Each letter of the alphabet is presented in uppercase and lowercase and begins the word of the item Pete eats. From accordion to camera to glue sticks and underpants, the childlike, thickly painted illustrations capture the whimsy and offbeat humor that describes the frazzled family and friends who lose these important items. The colors are strong and are as random and fun as the storyline itself. The witty conversational narrative is vocabulary-rich, including words like "iota," "kazoo," "livid," and "quadrillionth."
Grades Pre-K–2
Content Area Language Arts
Instructional Value Alliteration; descriptive writing; vocabulary
Text Structure Single letter (expanded)

Title *The Human Alphabet*
Author Philobolus
Illustrator John Kane
Publishing Company/Date Roaring Book Press/2005
ISBN# 978-1596430662
Summary The dance company Philobolus, composed of highly artistic dancer-athletes, created each letter of the alphabet using two or more dancers and then separately formed an

object that starts with that letter. For the letter A, two dancers in matching red leotards create the capital letter in the upper corner, and then three dancers combine their bodies to create an ant. Crisp photographs capture these cleverly composed human sculptures. An index in the back reviews the human alphabet and sculptures they created.

Grades Pre-K–2

Content Area Fine Arts

Instructional Value Observation and perception

Text Structure Hidden letter

Title *T Is for Tugboat: Navigating the Seas from A to Z*

Author Shoshanna Kirk

Illustrator Sara Gillingham

Publishing Company/Date Chronicle Books/2008

ISBN# 978-0811860499

Summary The maritime feel comes through in this mix of photographs, illustrations, and graphic images that float scrapbook-style on a woodgrain background. Each capital letter is in a vintage font and appears prominently in a corner of the page. At least three words are presented for each letter, and a phrase of explanation appears next to the object. There is a spread of knots and a page with Morse code. Phrases like "Ahoy," "Blow the Man Down," and "Heave Ho" are interspersed with words like "anchor," "buoy," and "hardtack." Other books in this series include *A Is for Astronaut: Exploring Space from A to Z* (2006) and *C Is for Caboose: Riding the Rails from A to Z* (2007).

Grades 3–6

Content Area Language Arts and Social Studies

Instructional Value Vocabulary; geography

Text Structure Single letter (expanded)

Title *On Market Street*

Author Arnold Lobel

Illustrator Anita Lobel

Publishing Company/Date Greenwillow Books/1981

ISBN# 978-0688803094

Summary Walking through a 17th-century market, a boy purchases gifts, each beginning with a letter of the alphabet. The capital letter and associated word are centered on the bottom of each page. Each item purchased multiplies and forms the body of the merchant who sells it. The apple merchant is created out of baskets brimming with red apples, and the ice cream merchant has arms made of ice cream cones and banana splits for shoes. The elaborately detailed and cleverly designed figures are a treat for the eyes as they help children associate these basic words with the letters of the alphabet.

Caldecott Honor Book

Grades Pre-K–2

Content Area Language Arts
Instructional Value Alphabetic principle
Text Structure Single letter

Title *Flora McDonnell's ABC*
Author/Illustrator Flora McDonnell
Publishing Company/Date Candlewick Press/1997
ISBN# 978-0763601188
Summary On a colorful background, each uppercase and lowercase letter is paired with two illustrations that offer a large and a small object associated with the letter. For the letter A, there is a large, crouching alligator (spelled in all uppercase letters) with small ants (spelled with all lowercase letters) walking along its snout. For T, a large tiger balances a tiny blue teapot between its ears. Although mostly animals, there are some non-animals depicted, like a car, a giant, a juggler, and a newspaper. The juxtapositions are witty, and the quiet balance between the disparate objects is amusing. Each of the objects is clearly identified, with the word written next to it.
Grades Pre-K–2
Content Area Language Arts
Instructional Value Alphabetic principle
Text Structure Single letter

Title *Peaceable Kingdom: The Shaker Abecedarius*
Author Shaker poem
Illustrator Alice and Martin Provenson
Publishing Company/Date Viking/1978
ISBN# 978-0670545001
Summary This alphabet rhyme taken from the July 1882 edition of the *Shaker Manifesto* is whimsical, bouncy, and full of unusual animal names. A large capital letter appears on the left side of each spread. Only the name of the first animal in the grouping begins with the featured letter: "Alligator, beetle, porcupine, whale," "Bobolink, panther, dragonfly, snail." The illustrations are carefully done, with the animals presented in an orderly fashion from left to right. Their precise black outlines and delicate coloring create a glimpse into the life of the Shakers, with the occasional figures churning butter or moving a wheelbarrow.
Grades Pre-K–2
Content Area Language Arts and Social Studies
Instructional Value Vocabulary; culture
Text Structure Single letter (expanded)

Title *The Handmade Alphabet*
Author/Illustrator Laura Rankin
Publishing Company/Date Turtleback/1996

ISBN# 978-0613005111

Summary Each page presents a letter in capital form in the upper left corner and then, with careful detail, a realistically portrayed hand demonstrates the manual alphabet used in American Sign Language. The hands are of many ages and ethnic backgrounds and engage with the object associated with the letter. The hand shape for the letter C allows for a delicate teacup to dangle on the thumb. A ribbon encircles the hand that signs the letter R. Although the word for the object is not written on each page (a list is in the back), the simplicity of the image—hand and object—makes it clear which object is referenced. Here the elegance of a gestural language is delicately detailed in color pencil illustrations.

Grades Pre-K–2

Content Area Language Arts

Instructional Value Vocabulary

Text Structure Single letter

Title *Dinosaur ABCs (Dinosaur School)*

Author/Illustrator Ava Saviola

Publishing Company/Date Gareth Stevens/2013

ISBN# 978-1433971358

Summary Charming cartoon baby dinosaurs engage with a range of alphabetical objects, from "A is for Ant" to "B is for Book," "C is for cup," and "D is for Doll." Letters are shown in both uppercase and lowercase. The jellybean-colored dinosaurs have friendly smiles and bright eyes. The dinosaur and object are set on a crisp white background, so there is no scenery to detract from the simple connection of letter and object.

Grades Pre-K–2

Content Area Language Arts

Instructional Value Alphabetic principle

Text Structure Single letter

Title *ABC Book of Early Americana*

Author/Illustrator Eric Sloane

Publishing Company/Date Dover Editions/2012

ISBN# 978-0486498089

Summary First published in 1963, these black-and-white pen-and-ink drawings depict objects commonplace in early American pioneer life but rarely seen today. Tools, house styles, and inventions are just a few of the topics. There is detail and elegance in the drawings, and the text harks back to a time when fine penmanship was prized. Each capital letter appears in a simple, drawn frame in an upper corner. It is associated with a word, and then numerous other examples are given, each with an illustration and a label and often with explanatory text. A few of the items shown for the letter A are "Axe," "Arm-rest," and "Apples" (including an apple butter pot, an apple butter paddle, and a Shaker apple drier).

Grades 3–6 and 7–12
Content Area Social Studies
Instructional Value Culture; history
Text Structure Single letter (expanded)

Title *A Is for Annabelle: A Doll's Alphabet*
Author/Illustrator Tasha Tudor
Publishing Company/Date Simon & Schuster Books for Young Readers/2001
ISBN# 978-0689828454
Summary Originally published in 1954, this book is a nostalgic look at two little girls wearing ruffled dresses and bows and playing with their grandmother's doll named Annabelle. Alternating spreads of color and black and white have the featured word on the left with a capital letter and a short continuation of the association on the right: "D is for Dresses we want her to wear." The girls play with an alphabetic array of doll-related items, from the box that holds her clothes, to her cloak, fan, gloves, shawl, and kerchiefs. A few words, like "nosegay," "overskirt," and "tippet," may be unfamiliar, but the sweet, flower-encircled drawings help to identify these delicate and treasured doll items.
Grades Pre-K–2
Content Area Language Arts
Instructional Value Alphabetic principle; vocabulary
Text Structure Single letter (expanded)

Title *Alphabet House*
Author/Illustrator Nancy Elizabeth Wallace
Publishing Company/Date Two Lions/2005
ISBN# 978-0761451921
Summary The book begins with an invitation to look inside the house of an adorable family of bunnies to see an alphabetical array of objects. Done with crisp, layered paper cutouts on primary-color backgrounds, each subsequent wordless scene depicts objects beginning with the featured letter. In the upper corner, the letter is presented in both uppercase and lowercase. A focus word for each letter appears as three identical objects along the top of the page. For A, there are three red apples, and for B, there are three baseballs. A listing of all objects to be found in each scene is in the back of the book.
Grades Pre-K–2
Content Area Language arts
Instructional Value Phonemic awareness
Text Structure Single letter

Title *Applebet: An ABC*
Author Clyde Watson
Illustrator Wendy Watson

Publishing Company/Date Farrar, Straus and Giroux/1982

ISBN# 978-0374404277

Summary The events at a small-town county fair are the backdrop for this alphabet book. The alphabet letter is capitalized in red, and its associated word is in boldface within the simple sentence. The sentences link together with simple rhymes to form a story. In addition to the alphabet, this book also includes "Soft C" (cider), "CH" (cherry), "Soft G" (gentleman), "QU" (quarrel), "SH" (sh-h!), "TH" (thief), and "WH" (whisper). The illustrations are outlined in fine black pen and carefully colored. A mother and child appear frequently throughout the story, as does the apple that is introduced on the first page.

Grades Pre-K–2

Content Area Language Arts

Instructional Value Phonemic awareness; rhyme and rhythm

Text Structure Single letter (expanded)

Poetry/Short Story

Title *Old Black Fly*

Author Jim Aylesworth

Illustrator Stephen Gammell

Publishing Company/Date Paw Prints/2009

ISBN# 978-1442004146

Summary A pesky and persistent housefly is on an alphabetical rampage, landing on people and the dog and getting into the birthday cake frosting and the noodle casserole. The catchy rhyme is brought to life through energetic and frenzied line illustrations full of splattered color, all lending to the sense of mayhem and annoyance that the fly brings. The capital letters are in a contrasting color and are not presented on their own; rather, they are embedded in the text. The emphatic swatting of the fly at the end is sure to please.

Grades Pre-K–2

Content Area Language Arts

Instructional Value Descriptive writing

Text Structure Single letter (expanded)

Title *Alphabet Juice*

Author Roy Blount Jr.

Publishing Company/Date Sarah Crichton Books/2008

ISBN# 978-0374103699

Summary A brilliant and hilarious alphabetical journey through the English language, exploring both letters and words. The alphabet provides the structure for this dictionary-like listing of a dozen or more words per letter, along with witty commentary on origins or usage. A few of the words from the chapter on the letter A are "abracadabra," "adverbial," "ain't," "arbitrary," and "as." The letters are presented in both capital and lowercase form. Also note a similar publication by this author, *Alpha Better Juice* (2011).

Grades 7–12

Content Area Language arts

Instructional Value Descriptive writing; grammar

Text Structure Conceptual text

Title *Ashley Bryan's ABC of African American Poetry*

Author/Illustrator Ashley Bryan

Publishing Company/Date Atheneum Books for Young Readers/1997

ISBN# 978-0689840456

Summary Selections from 25 powerful poems and one African American spiritual inspire a connection with each letter of the alphabet. Each tempera and gouache illustration swirls with color and captures the essence of the poem, even if the four or five lines of the poem written are only a part of the original poem. The letters appear framed in capital form in the upper left corner. The poets' names are included at the bottom of each page and include Langston Hughes, Gwendolyn Brooks, and Maya Angelou. The topics range from freedom and beauty to fate and spirit.

Grades 3–6

Content Area Language Arts and Social Studies

Instructional Value Descriptive writing; culture

Text Structure Conceptual text

Title *What I Hate from A to Z*

Author/Illustrator Roz Chast

Publishing Company/Date Bloomsbury USA/2011

ISBN# 978-1608196890

Summary This zany rant about common and not-so-common phobias and annoyances is ample subject for this alphabetical journey. Each letter begins the name of the subject(s) of a humorous and neurotic description. The illustrations are done in black-and-white pen and ink in the same style as Roz Chast's *New Yorker* cartoons. The alphabet letter is capitalized and appears as the start of the word and again within the illustration. Subjects covered include alien abduction, balloons, elevators, and quicksand.

Grades 7–12

Content Area Language Arts

Instructional Value Descriptive writing

Text Structure Single letter (expanded)

Title *Alphathoughts*

Author Lee Bennett Hopkins

Illustrator Marla Baggetta

Publishing Company/Date Wordsong/2003

ISBN# 978-1563979798

Summary Each capital letter is paired with a word in all capital letters. A brief, poetic phrase gives more depth to the word and is the subject of a jellybean-colored illustration that has a magical yet serene quality. The words are not the usual choices, and some poems are almost like riddles. For the letter L, the library is highlighted: "A pleasure place to ponder lifelong dreams."

Grades Pre-K–2

Content Area Language Arts

Instructional Value Descriptive writing; vocabulary

Text Structure Single letter (expanded)

Title *S Is for Story: A Writer's Alphabet*

Author Esther Hershenshorn

Illustrator Zachary Pullen

Publishing Company/Date Sleeping Bear Press/2009

ISBN# 978-1585364398

Summary This is an encouraging and inviting appeal to the young aspiring writer. Topics are covered clearly and include "alphabet," "character," "draft," "magic," and "revision." The letters are presented in both uppercase and lowercase and appear again at the start of a lyrical four-line poem. A side panel offers further detail and often includes an inspiring quote from a famous author. Caricature-like illustrations show kids using their imagination and enjoying the process of writing. An appendix offers additional interesting facts about famous authors.

Grades 3–6

Content Area Language Arts

Instructional Value Descriptive writing; rhyme and rhythm

Text Structure Conceptual text

Title *Once Upon an Alphabet: Short Stories for All the Letters*

Author/Illustrator Oliver Jeffers

Publishing Company/Date Philomel Books/2014

ISBN# 978-0399167911

Summary Connecting each letter to a word and then a story, this collection of short stories offers a variety and appeal to truly engage the young reader's imagination and intellect. Each page is full of surprises, from the whimsical to the slightly tragic. The ink and watercolor illustrations help evoke and set the mood. Each hand-drawn letter is presented on a separate colored page and then again in the story in uppercase and lowercase.

Grades 3–6

Content Area Language Arts

Instructional Value Descriptive writing

Text Structure Conceptual text

Title *L Is for Lollygag: Quirky Words for a Clever Tongue*
Author Tracy Sunrize Johnson
Illustrator Melinda Beck
Publishing Company/Date Chronicle Books/2008
ISBN# 978-0811860215
Summary This unique dictionary highlights words that are as fun to say as they are to read about. Each letter begins a chapter for dozens of words that begin with that letter. The capital letter is in a stylized font on a page by itself and then repeated at the top of each page of the word list. The pronunciation of each word is given along with a brief definition and an explanation, often as if the word were being described by a friend rather than a dictionary; for example, for "aficionado," it says, "Someone who is an expert on something, such as geography or toothpick collecting; if that someone is showing off his or her expertise, you can say (in a sarcastic way), 'Well, aren't you quite the aficionado!' " The red and black graphic illustrations lend an old-fashioned, quirky vibe.
Grades 7–12
Content Area Language Arts
Instructional Value Vocabulary
Text Structure Conceptual text

Title *Muddy As a Duck Puddle and Other American Similes*
Author Laurie Lawlor
Illustrator Ethan Long
Publishing Company/Date Holiday House/2010
ISBN# 978-0823423897
Summary Twenty-six sidesplitting and humorously folksy American expressions (or, more precisely, "proverbial expressions") form the backbone of this book. A bold capital letter begins each expression, including "Alike as two peas," "Busy as a stump-tailed cow in fly-time," and "Crooked as a barrel of snakes." An appendix explains the history of each expression, which often reflects the tall tales and exaggeration of characters like Paul Bunyan and Pecos Bill. The wide-eyed, cartoon-style illustrations bring to life the over-the-top, comical phrases.
Grades Pre-K–2
Content Area Language Arts and Social Studies
Instructional Value Vocabulary; culture; history
Text Structure Conceptual text

Title *S Is for Sea Glass: A Beach Alphabet*
Author Richard Michelson
Illustrator Doris Ettlinger
Publishing Company/Date Sleeping Bear Press/2014
ISBN# 978-1585368624

Summary The beauty and simple pleasures of time at the beach are shared in this alphabetical exploration. The capital letters are paired with focus words that become the topics of poems of varying length. The poetry is light and breezy and in a variety of styles. Some of the watercolor illustrations are in soft pastels, and others use strong, saturated colors. Topics include "castle," "gull," "horizon," "kite," "tide," and "wave."

Grades 3–6

Content Area Language Arts

Instructional Value Rhyme and rhythm

Text Structure Single letter (expanded)

Title *The Alphabet from A to Y with Bonus Letter Z!*

Author Steve Martin

Illustrator Roz Chast

Publishing Company/Date Flying Dolphin Press/2007

ISBN# 978-0385523776

Summary Twenty-six wildly imaginative, alliterative couplets prove ample inspiration for the detailed cartoon drawings that are completely off the wall. Each spread has a drawing on the left, and on the right is the featured capital letter, a small illustration of an item beginning with that letter, and an alliterative verse. Readers can linger over the text and then find the references in the drawing. Each reading will likely reveal more details and subtext.

Grades 3–6

Content Area Language Arts

Instructional Value Alliteration; descriptive writing

Text Structure Single letter (expanded)

Title *Edward Lear's A Was Once an Apple Pie*

Author/Illustrator Suse MacDonald

Publishing Company/Date Orchard Books/2005

ISBN# 978-0439660563

Summary This adaptation of Edward Lear's classic alphabet rhyme offers the same fun-to-say rhythm with more current word choices. Each capital letter is presented in a contrasting color and in boldface. What follows is an association with an object and then a rhyming riff of playful words, all of similar format: "A was once an apple pie, pidy, widy, tidy, pidy, nice insidy, apple pie!" The painted collage illustrations offer interesting textures and focus on the highlighted words, with limited other background details. Some spreads connect two words, such as the eel (for the letter E) that shares the scene with the fish (for the letter F).

Grades Pre-K–2

Content Area Language Arts

Instructional Value Rhyme and rhythm

Text Structure Single letter (expanded)

Title *Al Pha's Bet*
Author Amy Krouse Rosenthal
Illustrator Delphine Durand
Publishing Company/Date G. P. Putnam's Sons/ 2011
ISBN# 978-0399246012
Summary This entirely new take on the history of the alphabet begins with Al Pha, who bets that he can win the king's challenge to put the 26 recently invented letters in order. What follows is Al Pha's logic and the coincidences that lead him to create the present order, like putting the letter M in the middle because the word "middle" starts with M, or putting O after N so that there is "NO" giving up. Charming and quirky illustrations support the humorous text, which has an underlying theme of perseverance. The letters appear in capital form in multiple places but are consistently highlighted in the ever-growing string of letters that Al Pha puts together.
Grades Pre-K–2
Content Area Language Arts
Instructional Value Descriptive writing
Text Structure Single letter (expanded)

Title *Square Cat ABC*
Author/Illustrator Elizabeth Schoonmaker
Publishing Company/Date Aladdin/2014
ISBN# 978-1442498952
Summary In this charming tale, a friendly mouse encourages the square cat Eula to try some spinach. For the letters A through D, the sentences "Amazing! A big square cat is digging in the dirt!" string over three spreads, making this book literally a page-turner. The large red letters of the alphabet are either uppercase or lowercase, depending on where they fall within the sentence. Children will find the humor in the square cat's reluctance to try spinach. A simple white background allows the colorful watercolors to pop.
Grades Pre-K–2
Content Area Language Arts
Instructional Value Descriptive writing
Text Structure Single letter

Title *To Do: A Book of Alphabets and Birthdays*
Author Gertrude Stein
Illustrator Giselle Potter
Publishing Company/Date Yale University Press/2011
ISBN# 978-0300170979
Summary In this musing compilation of tales, each letter of the alphabet is associated with four names of both real and imagined people who are the subject of a short story told

in verse. The unique and random narrative refers to their birthdays and other reflections. The letters of the alphabet appear colorful, bold, and slightly askew within the text. Illustrations combine folk art and surreal elements, bringing the magic of Gertrude Stein's words to life.

Grades 7–12
Content Area Language Arts
Instructional Value Descriptive writing
Text Structure Conceptual text

Title R Is for Rhyme: A Poetry Alphabet
Author Judy Young
Illustrator Victor Juhasz
Publishing Company/Date Sleeping Bear Press/2005
ISBN# 978-1585362400
Summary Sharing the wide breadth of poetic possibilities (including acrostic, ballad, haiku, and iambic), this book shares sample poems that illustrate poetic tools, terms, and techniques as well as a narrative that explains the history of the poem form and helps the reader understand the meaning. A question at the end of the narrative encourages a repeated and more careful reading of the poem. The letters are presented in capital and lowercase form and again in capital form to introduce the type of poem. The colored pencil illustrations are energetic, expressive, and humorous and bring to life the everyday topics of the poems, making poetry even more accessible and relatable.

Grades 3–6 and 7–12
Content Area Language Arts
Instructional Value Descriptive writing; rhyme and rhythm
Text Structure Conceptual text

Science

Title *Jumbo Minds' Science ABCs: ABCs of Chemistry*
Author A. C. Lemonwood
Illustrator David Cowles
Publishing Company/Date Jumbo Minds, Inc./2015
ISBN# 978-1944049058
Summary This book introduces the language and concepts of chemistry, from atom to zinc. The left side of each spread presents the capital and lowercase letter in an upper corner. The featured word is introduced with a short, clear definition followed by a few sentences with further detail. Featured words and short definitions include "atom" ("a tiny bit of matter") and "bond" ("link between atoms"). The crisp, colorful illustrations, presented on the right page of each spread, are friendly and succinct, with a small dash of humor.

Grades Pre-K–2 and 3–6
Content Area Science
Instructional Value Chemistry
Text Structure Single letter (expanded)

Title *Jumbo Minds' Science ABCs: ABCs of Biology*
Author A. C. Lemonwood
Illustrator David Cowles
Publishing Company/Date Jumbo Minds, Inc./2015
ISBN# 978-1944049096
Summary This book introduces the language and concepts of biology, from "abdomen" to "zooplankton." The left side of each spread presents the capital and lowercase letter in an upper corner. The featured word is introduced with a short, clear definition followed by a few sentences with further detail. Featured words and short definitions include "abdomen" ("belly") and "bacteria" ("one-celled life forms"). The crisp, colorful illustrations, presented on the right page of each spread, are friendly and succinct, with a small dash of humor.
Grades Pre-K–2 and 3–6
Content Area Science
Instructional Value Life science
Text Structure Single letter (expanded)

Title *Jumbo Minds' Science ABCs: ABCs of Earth Science*
Author A. C. Lemonwood
Illustrator David Cowles
Publishing Company/Date Jumbo Minds, Inc./2015
ISBN# 978-1944049010
Summary This book introduces the language and concepts of earth science, from "asteroid" to "zephyr." The left side of each spread presents the capital and lowercase letter in an upper corner. The featured word is introduced with a short, clear definition followed by a few sentences with further detail. Featured words and short definitions include "biome" ("life zone") and "soil" ("Earth's skin"). The crisp, colorful illustrations, presented on the right page of each spread, are friendly and succinct, with a small dash of humor.
Grades Pre-K–2 and 3–6
Content Area Science
Instructional Value Earth science
Text Structure Single letter (expanded)

Title *Jumbo Minds' Science ABCs: ABCs of Physics*
Author A.C. Lemonwood
Illustrator David Cowles

Publishing Company/Date Jumbo Minds, Inc./2015

ISBN# 978-1944049133

Summary This book introduces the language and concepts of physics, from "acceleration" to "absolute zero." The left side of each spread presents the capital and lowercase letter in an upper corner. The featured word is introduced with a short, clear definition followed by a few sentences with further detail. Featured words and short definitions include "acceleration" ("speeding up, slowing down, turning") and "buoyancy" ("floating force"). The crisp, colorful illustrations, presented on the right page of each spread, are friendly and succinct, with a small dash of humor.

Grades Pre-K–2 and 3–6

Content Area Science

Instructional Value Physics

Text Structure Single letter (expanded)

Title *W Is for Wind: A Weather Alphabet*

Author Pat Michaels

Illustrator Melanie Rose

Publishing Company/Date Sleeping Bear Press/2005

ISBN# 978-1585363308

Summary The subject of weather and its impact on our daily lives provides ample material for this alphabetic tour. Topics include "atmosphere," "barometer," "cloud," "lightning," "ozone," and "vapor." The letters are presented in both uppercase and lowercase and appear again at the start of a lyrical four-line poem ("W is for Wind. It flows south, north, east and west./The wind is never really at rest./The world depends on its constant ebb and flow./Without the wind the weather would have nowhere to go"). Colorful, detailed, painted illustrations clearly present the topic words.

Grades 3–6

Content Area Language Arts and Science

Instructional Value Rhyme and rhythm; earth science

Text Structure Conceptual text

Title *W Is for Waves: An Ocean Alphabet*

Authors Marie and Roland Smith

Illustrator John Megahan

Publishing Company/Date Sleeping Bear Press/2008

ISBN# 978-1585362547

Summary This deep dive into the mysterious and fascinating world of oceans covers subjects from mythology to ocean animals and ocean features. The letters are presented in both uppercase and lowercase and appear again at the start of a lyrical four-lined poem. Topics range from "Atlantis," "beach," and "camouflage" to "tides," "volcanoes," and "waves," each supported with a compelling narrative that is rich with detail and vocabulary. The illustrations capture the sparkle of light on the water's surface as well as the deep blues and grays of the water at varying depths.

Grades 3–6

Content Area Language Arts and Science

Instructional Value Rhyme and rhythm; earth science

Text Structure Conceptual text

Title *B Is for Blue Planet: An Earth Science Alphabet*

Author Ruth Strother

Illustrator Robert Marstall

Publishing Company/Date Sleeping Bear Press/2011

ISBN# 978-1585364541

Summary The discoveries and mysteries of our Planet Earth offer a wide variety of alphabetical topics, including "coral reef," "earthquakes," "fossils," "northern lights," "water cycle," and "zones." The letters are presented in both uppercase and lowercase and appear again at the start of a lyrical four-line poem. The illustrations include labeled diagrams (for plate tectonics and the earth's mantle, for example) as well as illustrations that capture the extreme forces of nature. A "Facts Page" discusses climate change and other earth facts.

Grades 3–6

Content Area Language Arts and Science

Instructional Value Rhyme and rhythm; earth science

Text Structure Conceptual text

Title *S Is for Scientist: A Discovery Alphabet*

Author Larry Verstraete

Illustrator David Geister

Publishing Company/Date Sleeping Bear Press/2010

ISBN# 978-1585364701

Summary The important steps of the scientific process and the wonders of learning and experimentation are presented in this book. Topics include "build," "compare," "demonstrate," "experiment," "hypothesize," "measure," and "prove." The letters are presented in both uppercase and lowercase and appear again at the start of a lyrical four-line poem. Detailed painted illustrations show people at moments of discovery. A "You, the Scientist" page offers four experiments for the budding physicist, chemist, microbiologist, and environmental scientist.

Grades 3–6

Content Area Language Arts and Science

Instructional Value Rhyme and rhythm; chemistry; earth science; life science; physics

Text Structure Conceptual text

Transportation

Title *Z Goes Home*
Author/Illustrator Jon Agee
Publishing Company/Date Michael di Capua Books/2003
ISBN# 978-0786819874
Summary The large, red letter Z leaves its spot at the sign at the City Zoo and makes its long trek home, through city and country, encountering 26 interesting things along the way. Each page shows a letter of the alphabet in capital form, but altered in some way to become the object it describes. The A is green and has feet and antennae, forming an alien. The capital B lies on its back to form a bridge. The woodpile is shaped to form the letter W. Tucked within the scenery, one can see a glimpse of the red letter Z as it makes its way home to a family of red letters. The illustrations are loosely drawn and use large areas of soft color. A brief definition of each of the objects is in the back of the book.
Grades Pre-K–2
Content Area Language Arts
Instructional Value Vocabulary
Text Structure Hidden letter

Title *ABCDrive! A Car Trip Alphabet*
Author/Illustrator Naomi Howland
Publishing Company/Date Clarion Books/1994
ISBN# 978-0618040346
Summary A young boy and his mother take a car trip from the city to the country. With all of the cars and activity on the road, it is easy to follow this boy, because his yellow balloon trails out the window of their red car. The fine colored-pencil illustrations with lots of details (the baby blowing bubbles from the apartment window, the child in a wheelchair crossing the street, the bride and groom getting photographed near the lake) are loosely based on the San Francisco area. The capital letter is framed in a yellow box and is next to the single featured word. Words include "ambulance," "bus," "cement mixer," "jeep," "limousine," and "traffic." Although the featured word is represented in the illustration, it takes a keen young eye to find it.
Grades Pre-K–2
Content Area Language Arts
Instructional Value Alphabetic principle
Text Structure Single letter

Title *Backseat A-B-See*
Author/Illustrator Maria van Lieshout
Publishing Company/Date Chronicle Books LLC/2012

ISBN# 978-1452106649

Summary For children who love books about transportation, or who are headed on a road trip, this book offers examples of road signs in vivid color for each letter. On a glossy black background, a dotted line runs across the spread to represent the road itself. The uppercase letter is paired with a recognizable road sign; examples include "airport," "bike route," "stop," and "van accessible."

Grades Pre-K–2

Content Area Social Studies

Instructional Value Geography

Text Structure Single letter

Title *All Aboard! A Traveling Alphabet*

Author/ Illustrator Bill Mayer

Publishing Company/Date Margaret K. McElderry Books/2008

ISBN# 978-0689852497

Summary With a clear nod to classic travel posters, this book's bold graphic illustrations are perfectly and simply composed. Each letter is cleverly hidden within a close-up or from an unusual viewing angle of the many types of transportation. A single word (in varying typeface) is placed on the image. Readers are invited to find the letter D on the page with the word "Dock." Each letter becomes an integral part of the illustration, so that young children, who will want to trace the letter once they find it, will be making large and purposeful movements.

Grades Pre-K–2

Content Area Fine Arts

Instructional Value Graphic design; observation and perception

Text Structure Hidden letter

Title *Mazeways A to Z*

Author/Illustrator Roxie Munro

Publishing Company/Date Sterling Publishing Co., Inc./2007

ISBN# 978-1402737749

Summary Composed of over 700 hidden objects, these astonishing and truly engaging mazes are each based in form on a capital letter of the alphabet, which is then associated with a word like "circus" or "ranch" to set the stage for the fun. Follow the instructions to navigate the brightly colored, challenging mazes and find the many objects within the maze. Adults and children alike will be thoroughly intrigued. An answer key in the back highlights the path and the hidden objects.

Grades 3–6

Content Area Social Studies

Instructional Value Geography

Text Structure Hidden letter

Title *ABC's on Wings*
Author/Illustrator Ramon Olivera
Publishing Company/Date Little Simon/2015
ISBN# 978-1481432429
Summary From "Aa is for ace" to "Zz is for zeppelin," this book will be a treat for young aviation lovers. Bold, retro-styled graphic illustrations show a variety of flying machines soaring through the sky. The sense of movement is emphasized with stylized arrows or lines. Both professional pilots and children with their toy gliders are depicted. Each letter is displayed in both uppercase and lowercase and is associated with a word related to flight. Most words are simple, like "engines" and "fuel"; other words may be less familiar, like "ace," "intake" and "tailwind."
Grades Pre-K–2
Content Area Fine Arts and Social Studies
Instructional Value Graphic design; geography
Text Structure Single letter

Title *The Airplane Alphabet Book*
Authors Jerry Pallotta and Fred Stillwell
Illustrator Rob Bolster
Publishing Company/Date Charlesbridge/1997
ISBN# 978-0881069075
Summary Packed with vintage airplanes and full of the allure and fascination of flight, this book provides detailed illustrations of planes in flight against a variety of backdrops. At times, it is as if the reader is in flight too, due to the perspective used for the illustrations. Each uppercase and lowercase letter is clearly presented, and the text offers description and inspiration for young aviators. There are many other alphabet books created by Jerry Pallotta, covering a wide range of topics.
Grades 3–6
Content Area Social Studies
Instructional Value History
Text Structure Conceptual text

Title *Alphabeep: A Zipping, Zooming ABC*
Author Debora Pearson
Illustrator Edward Miller
Publishing Company/Date Holiday House/2003
ISBN# 978-0823417223
Summary Busy roadways full of cars, trucks, ambulances, and dump trucks combine with road signs and the beeps, honks, and screeches of transportation noises. Each colorful alphabet letter is presented in uppercase and lowercase and is associated with a transportation word from "ambulance" to "zamboni." A brief narrative describes the scene.

Graphic, brightly colored illustrations add energy to the busy and active roads. The usefulness of each vehicle is shown: the utility truck repairs the telephone wires, and the wrecking crane takes down a building.

Grades Pre-K–2

Content Area Language Arts and Social Studies

Instructional Value Descriptive writing; geography

Text Structure Single letter (expanded)

Title *Race from A to Z*

Author Jon Scieszka

Illustrator Dani Jones

Publishing Company/Date Simon & Schuster Books for Young Readers/2014

ISBN# 978-1416941361

Summary Jack the truck invites all of his truck friends to race all the way to Z. Each eager vehicle, from construction types to fire engines to monster trucks, has a big personality and is eager to win. There is a lot of action and movement, and the colorful, high-energy illustrations capture the spinning wheels of the jumps as these trucks head to the finish line. The letters are presented as capitals in contrasting colors, and each one begins an alliterative sentence that rhymes with the sentence on the facing page. End pages give a snapshot and a name for each of these truck characters.

Grades Pre-K–2

Content Area Language Arts

Instructional Value Alphabetic principle; phonemic awareness

Text Structure Single letter (expanded)

Title *B Is for Bulldozer: A Construction ABC*

Author June Sobel

Illustrator Melissa Iwai

Publishing Company/Date Gulliver Books/2003

ISBN# 978-0152022501

Summary Families observe a busy construction site over several months to watch as each new piece of equipment comes in to help build the amusement park the community can enjoy at the conclusion. Each colorful featured letter is in capital form and begins a word in a sentence. Sometimes the letter begins the sentence, and at other times it is embedded within the sentence. The illustrations are sweet but also full of detail that will delight those who love construction vehicles. A rich vocabulary is introduced, with words like "asphalt," "excavator," "I-beam," and "scaffolds."

Grades Pre-K–2

Content Area Language Arts

Instructional Value Rhyme and rhythm

Text Structure Single letter (expanded)

Title *Alphabet Trains*

Author Samantha R. Vamos

Illustrator Ryan O'Rourke

Publishing Company/Date Charlesbridge/2015

ISBN# 978-1580895927

Summary Trains, in alphabetic array—from "auto" and "bullet" to "Victoria Express" and "Zephyr"—are shown in their appropriate landscapes, whether hugging a side of a mountain or carting coal from a mine. The subdued palette of the illustrations is punctuated with more colorful treatment of the trains. Each illustration includes the featured letter, enlarged and part of the landscape; for example, for the letter R, several large R's are drawn as if made of wood and stand amid the tall pine trees next to the *Rocky Mountaineer* train. This offers opportunities to find the letter in both capital and lowercase form. The bouncy, rhyming text is composed of a sentence for each train: "E is for elevated train, cruising on raised tracks. F is for freight train, hauling goods piled in stacks."

Grades Pre-K–2

Content Area Language Arts

Instructional Value Rhyme and rhythm

Text Structure Hidden letter

Title *Alphabet Trucks*

Author Samantha R. Vamos

Illustrator Ryan O'Rourke

Publishing Company/Date Charlesbridge/2013

ISBN# 978-1580894289

Summary This is a perfect book for a truck lover. Twenty-six different hardworking trucks are highlighted with illustrations that show them in action and with simple, rhyming verse. The letters of the alphabet are used to begin each verse, and, when multiplied, the letters become the cargo in the box truck or the items in the back of the recycle truck. Children and adults form the fabric of the community served by these trucks, and the trucks' benefits are made clear.

Grades Pre-K–2

Content Area Language Arts

Instructional Value Rhyme and rhythm

Text Structure Hidden letter

Urban

Title *B Is for Brooklyn*

Author/Illustrator Selina Alko

Publishing Company/Date Henry Holt and Co./2012

ISBN# 978-0905092134

Summary This celebratory tribute to a popular borough of New York City showcases its diverse population and its wealth of sites, activities, and food. Beginning with a city map, each uppercase letter is associated with a word like "Brooklyn Bridge" or "Coney Island." Numerous additional words round out the scene and give a true taste of what locals know and love—words like "baseball," "egg creams," and "the F Train." The gouache and collage illustrations lend to the energy and vibrancy of the book.

Grades Pre-K–2

Content Area Social Studies

Instructional Value Culture

Text Structure Single letter

Title *Welcome to My Neighborhood!*

Author Quiara Algería Hudes

Illustrator Shino Arihara

Publishing Company/Date Arthur A. Levine Books/2010

ISBN# 978-0545094245

Summary A young girl takes her friend on a tour of her city neighborhood, sharing its simple pleasures, like the spray of a fire hydrant and the delicious smells of dinners cooking. Each letter is presented in capital form and is associated with part of the community. Many of the words are uniquely associated with lower economic urban communities, like "abandoned car," "graffiti," and "a plastic crate for a basketball hoop." The illustrations, with their gray concrete backgrounds, support the depiction of the environment. The pops of color come from the people and their vibrancy. There are a few Spanish words, like "abuelo" (grandmother) and "quemar" (to burn).

Grades Pre-K–2

Content Area Social Studies

Instructional Value Culture

Text Structure Single letter (expanded)

Title *NYC ABC*

Author/Illustrator The Metropolitan Museum of Art

Publishing Company/Date Skira Rizzoli/2011

ISBN# 978-0847837014

Summary This is a thorough introduction to the great places and spaces of New York City, through images from the collection of the Metropolitan Museum of Art. Painting, photographs, and prints by world-famous artists populate each entry of the alphabet. From "avenue" to "zeppelin," the energy and unique charm of the city are captured. Each capital letter is paired with a word or phrase ("B is for Brooklyn Bridge" or "N is for New York at night") and accompanied by two to four images. A thumbnail checklist with identifying information for each work of art is in the back of the book.

Grades Pre-K–2
Content Area Fine Arts
Instructional Value Observation and perception
Text Structure Single letter

Title *I Stink!*
Author Kate McMullan
Illustrator Jim McMullan
Publishing Company/Date HarperCollins/2002
ISBN# 978-006029849
Summary With a big personality and an even bigger appetite, this tough-talking garbage truck boasts of its strength as it prepares to do its nightly job: to eat all of the city's trash. An alphabet soup of unappetizing items follows, each with its own yuck factor (dirty diapers, fish heads, gobs of gum, moldy meatballs, nasty neckties, and year-old yams). The initial letter of the alphabetical item is uppercase and in a contrasting color. The illustrations are bold and colorful, personifying the garbage truck further by depicting dark eyes in the windshield and a large, toothy grin along the bumper.
Grades Pre-K–2
Content Area Language Arts
Instructional Value Alliteration; vocabulary
Text Structure Single letter

Chapter 6

Alphabet Books and English Language Learners (ELLs)

> *We breathe in our first language, and swim in our second.*
> Adam Gopnik

English Language Learners

It will come as no surprise to any educator that our public schools now serve millions of international students as well as children from immigrant parents (Pitcher and Mackey; Reutzel and Cooter). Representing 11 percent of America's 49.5 million public school students, English Language Learners (ELLs) can be found in almost every school district or county. California leads the nation with the most ELL students (1.1 million), while Texas ranks second (Pitcher and Mackey). The importance of devoting an entire chapter to the curricular and instructional needs of English Language Learners cannot be overstated.

According to the Migration Policy Institute Web site, "Spanish is the most common first or home language, spoken by 71 percent of ELL students." Specifically, this chapter presents information, alphabet books, Web sites, and other resources for the Spanish-speaking English learners in our schools today.

Instructional Support for ELLs

Instructional support for English Language Learners centers on two themes: (1) language and cultural identity and (2) English language acquisition. "Building on the literacy skills that the second language learner brings from home affirms both his native language and his culture" (Pitcher and Mackey, p. 157). In addition, researchers conclude that "language-minority students who become literate in their first language are likely to have an advantage in the acquisition of English literacy" (Reutzel and Cooter, p. 126).

Cultural Identity and Alphabet Books

As English Language Learners strive to learn English to succeed in academic settings, their desire to value their cultural identities remains strong. Several alphabet books accentuate a specific culture, affirming its traditions and values. In *Once Around the Block,* Loranzo paints vivid, warm pictures of the people who live in a Mexican American neighborhood. The book portrays Benito and his love of big bean burritos and jicama, and readers can relate their lives and their communities to the characters so lovingly depicted. In *N Is for Navidad,* authors Elya, Banks, and Cepeda depict Latino Christmas customs, such as chilies for decoration and delicious *buñuelos.*

Vocabulary and Alphabet Books

Explicit teaching of vocabulary, especially within the academic content areas, remains the essential instructional goal for all teachers of English Language Learners (Pitcher and Mackey; Reutzel and Cooter). Alphabet books serve as outstanding supplementary texts due to their usually abbreviated text and inclusion of many illustrations. "Since alphabet books are not text-heavy and rely upon illustrations to inform the reader, they interest the reluctant reader while still providing information" (Jennifer Sommer Web site).

Bilingual Vocabulary Frames

A vocabulary frame is an instructional strategy that presents several cues to the student to aid in the comprehension of a conceptual vocabulary term (e.g., photosynthesis). In the four-step process, students (1) define the word being studied, (2) create a non-example of the word, (3) use the word in a silly sentence, and (4) draw a picture that goes with the silly sentence. Associating a word with its non-example remains one of the most effective strategies for learning a new term (Blanchfield and Tompkins). Using the word in a silly sentence engages the learner in a personal, amusing way, and kinesthetic learners will be aided by drawing a picture of the silly sentence.

In the bilingual vocabulary frame, the four-step process is completed in both English and Spanish. By connecting the student's personal schema through the student-created graphic and the creation of

Figure 6.1   Bilingual Vocabulary Frame

a silly sentence using the target word, students retain the word's meaning. Teachers present examples of vocabulary frames with easily comprehended words.

Materials
Vocabulary frame template
Twenty-six English words, especially within content areas

To begin, teachers present examples of vocabulary frames in English and Spanish with easily comprehended words. Next, each student draws an English word from a paper bag. Each student completes the bilingual vocabulary frame for the chosen word. Bilingual vocabulary frames are posted on classroom walls or in long hallways in alphabetical order. Please see figure 6.1 for a photograph of a completed bilingual vocabulary frame using "summer" as the target English word.

Cognates and Alphabet Books

Cognate instruction provides an easily traveled bridge from English to Spanish and then for the return trip from Spanish to English. Cognates fall into two categories: true cognates and false cognates/false friends (Spanish Cognates Web site). Constituting about 90 percent of English–Spanish cognates, true cognates share the same Latin root and look and sound the same. True cognates have the same meaning and thus provide English Language Learners with a powerful tool for comprehending academic concepts (Reutzel and Cooter). Examples of true Spanish–English cognates include "bank/*banco*" and "inform/*informar.*" On the other hand, English–Spanish false cognates (false friends) look and sound the same but have different meanings. An example of a false English–Spanish cognate would be the Spanish word *embarasada*, which in English looks and sounds like "embarrassed." In Spanish, however, that word means "pregnant"! Vocabulary instruction for English Language Learners stresses the difference between true cognates and false cognates. Presenting several true cognates in *ABeCedarios: Mexican Folk Art ABCs in English and Spanish*, Cynthia Weill reinforces the similarities between certain words in English and in Spanish. Cognates support ELLs in both their everyday oral communications and academic readings.

True Cognate Alphabet Book

This instructional activity teaches about true English–Spanish cognates. By selecting the topic (encourage students to choose a broad, general topic, such as transportation, food, or school) for their book, students can exhibit personal choice in creating their true cognate alphabet book. Student choice of assignments enhances motivation and a desire to succeed.

Materials
Computer access for English–Spanish cognates
Twenty-seven pages of cardstock or construction paper (1 page for title) for paper book OR
Create a digital true cognate alphabet book

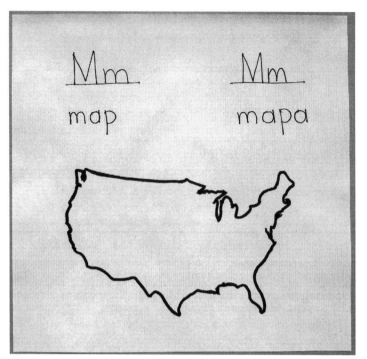

Figure 6.2   Page from Cognate Alphabet Book

Each student or small group of students will choose a topic as the theme of their alphabet book. Students will visit English–Spanish cognate Web Sites to find 26 true cognates to incorporate within their alphabet book.

Completed true cognate alphabet books can be displayed in the school library or uploaded to the school or classroom Web site. Please see figure 6.2 for a photograph of one page from a true cognate alphabet book, featuring the letter M.

Dual Language Alphabet Books

Using dual language books within all classrooms, and specifically within ESL (English as a Second Language) programs, supports the ELL student in learning second language vocabulary for everyday communication. As these students progress in their language development and confidence, dual language books provide support in academic areas. By containing words in both languages, dual language books offer a kind of "sheltered instruction" that promotes English language development while presenting academic concepts in understandable terms for ELLs (Echevarria, Vost, and Short). In addition, dual language books foster pride in one's cultural background, giving students that essential sense of self-worth and cultural identity. Within the vividly golden pages of *Gathering the Sun: An Alphabet in Spanish and English* (2011), Alma Flor Ada depicts vegetables, trees, flowers, and other aspects of nature in four- or five-line poems in Spanish first and then in English. Placing the two languages on adjoining pages reinforces the written translations, which is essential for visual learners. Warm, endearing illustrations present a sense of cultural pride that showcases hard work and community. In a similar fashion, Stephanie Maze describes a large amount of action and sports vocabulary in her dual language book, *Keeping Fit from A to Z: Mantente En Forma de la A a la Z* (2014). Through presenting the English version sometimes first and on other pages the Spanish language first, neither language is given priority. The book concludes with eight pages of facts and trivia about sports, activities, and keeping healthy.

Dual Language Alphabet Book

This instructional activity links English and Spanish through the student creation of a dual language alphabet book. Allowing English Language Learners to work within groups and to choose a topic of interest to research and write about will enhance student motivation.

Materials

Twenty-seven pages of cardstock or construction paper (1 page for the cover)

A variety of art materials (markers, colored pencils, etc.)

As a class, students will decide upon a broad topic as the theme of a dual language alphabet book. Within groups or individually, students will choose an alphabet letter and research possible topics (in either English or Spanish) that begin with their chosen letter. The use of dual language Web sites and books is strongly encouraged. Each student or group of students will create one page in a dual language alphabet book. Please see figure 6.3 for a photograph of one page from a dual language book.

Today is my grandfather's birthday. My family is going to celebrate at my house this evening. My mom baked his favorite chocolate cake, and I have made him a special card. My grandfather was an architect and retired this year. He now has more time to spend with me, and we are planning a trip to New York City to see the Empire State Building.

Hoy es el cumpleaños de mi abuelo. Mi familia se va a celebrar en mi casa esta noche. Mi madre al horno su pastel de chocolate favorito, y yo le hice una tarjeta especial. Mi abuelo fue un arquitecto y se retiró este año. Ahora tiene más tiempo para estar conmigo, y estamos planeando un viaje a Nueva York para ver el edificio del Empire State.

Figure 6.3   Page from Dual Language Book

English Language Proficiency Standards

According to the Web site of the international association Teachers of English to Speakers of Other Languages (TESOL), five levels of English language proficiency have been delineated. The use of five levels reflects the complexity of language development and also enables educators to track student progress across grade levels with the same scale. Likewise, on the Teachers First Web site, five levels of English language proficiency are depicted. Although the headings of each of the five levels vary from one Web site to another, the defining characteristics that profile student behaviors and language acquisition remain very similar.

Listed below are brief summaries of five levels of English language proficiency:

Level 1: Beginning (Starting)

This student has a very limited vocabulary in English and may not understand the American classroom and its participatory style. She or he lacks oral comprehension of English and is thus unable to follow simple directions or complete assignments.

Level 2: High Beginning (Emerging)

This student can respond to some oral directions and may attempt to complete simple classroom assignments. She or he still possesses a limited vocabulary and recognizes only very commonly used words and phrases. The student enjoys extra attention from teachers and other students while appreciating lots of guidance and instructional support.

Level 3: Intermediate (Developing)

This student shows more confidence in his or her ability to respond to classroom questions and complete written assignments. Vocabulary support is still needed, especially in written work. This student understands and can communicate using everyday words and phrases.

Level 4: High Intermediate (Expanding)

This student's command of the English language shows great comprehension and understanding. Vocabulary has expanded, and the student can participate in classroom and social activities with confidence. Grammar errors are infrequent now.

Level 5: Advanced (Bridging)

This student is able to function, both in oral and written communications, near grade level. His or her writing skills show accurate grammar and syntax, although a dictionary may be needed for confirmation of more complex terms. This student can, and usually does, excel in academic endeavors due to his or her strong motivation to succeed (Teachers First Web site; Teachers of English to Speakers of Other Languages Web site).

Alphabet Books for ELLs and Summaries

Utilizing the five levels of English language proficiency described above to select the readability level of the text, the following alphabet books for English Language Learners are presented:

Title *Gathering the Sun: An Alphabet in Spanish and English*
Author Alma Flor Ada
Illustrator Simón Silva
Publishing Company/Date HarperCollins/1997
ISBN# 978-0688139049
Summary In this bilingual book, expressive four- or five-line poems, written in Spanish and then translated into English, share the bounty of fruits, vegetables, and fields tended to with pride by Hispanic farmworkers. Each capital letter begins a Spanish word, followed by the rhyming text. The painted illustrations use warm, sun-drenched colors, and the textures of the visible brushstrokes highlight the strength and hard work of the people. Poem topics include *árboles* (trees), *betabel* (beet), César Chávez, *gracias* (thanks), and *querer* (love).
ELP Level 3 (intermediate or developing)
Content Area Language Arts
Instructional Value Vocabulary
Text Structure Single letter (expanded)

Title *N Is for Navidad*
Author/Illustrator Susan Middleton Elya, Merry Banks, and Joe Cepeda
Publishing Company/Date Chronicle Books/2007
ISBN# 978-0811852050
Summary A rhythmic text, coupled with vibrant oil paintings, conveys the joys of a Latino Christmas season. This bilingual book includes traditions and religious significance from Christmas through Three Kings' Day. The multigenerational family is depicted with broad smiles and bright eyes, enjoying the delicious food and playful moments with each other. Each capital letter is associated with a Spanish word that is explained in English. There is a page for the Spanish digraphs CH and LL and the letter Ñ (*chiles, llegada,* and *niño*). Other Spanish words include *àngel, buñuelos, campanas, kilómetros, risas,* and *zapatos.*
ELP Level 2 (high beginning or emerging)
Content Area Language Arts and Social Studies

Instructional Value Rhythm and rhyme; culture
Text Structure Single letter (expanded)

Title *Animales de la A a la Z: Animals from A to Z*
Author João Coutinhas
Illustrator Pedro Pinto
Publishing Company/Date Everest/2005
ISBN# 978-8444142456
Summary The animal name appears first in English, beginning with a capital letter, followed by the Spanish name below. The neighboring page has a simple, informative sentence, such as, "Alligators live in rivers and swamps." This is followed by the Spanish translation, such as, "*Los caimanes viven en ríos y pantanos.*" There is a humorous quality to the childlike outlines of the animals, each colored with vibrant hues and bearing similar circular eyes. A few of the animal names are cognates, such as "flamingo/ *flamenco.*"
ELP Level 2 (high beginning or emerging)
Content Area Science
Instructional Value Life science
Text Structure Single letter (expanded)

Title *A Is for Airplane: A Es para Avión*
Author Theresa Howell
Illustrator David Brooks
Publishing Company/Date Cooper Square Publishing/2003
ISBN# 978-0873588317
Summary This brightly colored, bilingual board book will help young children learn their ABCs in both Spanish and English. Each uppercase and lowercase letter is associated with a single commonplace object. The object is illustrated in a friendly cartoon manner with bright colors and simple features. The English description is written on the top of the page ("Aa is for Airplane"), and the Spanish is written below ("Aa es para Avión"). Some of the words are cognates.
ELP Level 1 (beginning or starting)
Content Area Language Arts
Instructional Value Alphabetic principle; phonemic awareness
Text Structure Single letter

Title *Once Around the Block: Una Vuelta a la Manzana*
Author/Illustrator Jóse Lozano
Publishing Company/Date Cinco Puntos Press/2009
ISBN# 978-1933693576
Summary Vivid short narratives for the letters of the alphabet give a glimpse into a Mexican American community. The narrative is presented first in English, using many names

of people and key words that begin with the featured letter. Beginning with Amelia and Anita, sisters who argue, and Benito, who loves baseball, bumblebees, and big bean burritos, each paragraph goes further to offer other charming details. The paragraph is then translated in Spanish. All of the letters are in capital form and the Ñ, LL, and CH are also given one page together. The vibrant drawings are vignettes of the life of each of the people. Composed of warm colors associated with Mexican art, the painted illustrations appear as if photographs, with white deckle edges and corner adhesions.

ELP Level 3 (intermediate or developing)

Content Area Language Arts and Social Studies

Instructional Value Alliteration; culture

Text Structure Single letter

Title *Healthy Foods from A to Z/Comida Sana de la A a la Z*

Author Stephanie Maze

Photographer Renée Comet

Publishing Company/Date Moonstone Press LLC/2012

ISBN# 978-0983498315

Summary This bilingual picture book features appealing photographs of seven or so fruits, vegetables, grains, or dairy foods that begin with each letter of the alphabet. The names are given in English and Spanish, and then the items are playfully combined to create a unique and expressive face (spiky hair is made out of ochre, an orange twist becomes an earring, a vanilla bean serves as a nose). A template in the back of the book has instructions in both languages on how to make a Healthy Food Face, as well as other healthy food projects. A comprehensive listing of all of the foods features a thumbnail sketch for each food, along with a description of its nutritional value and information on where it is grown.

ELP Level 1 (beginning or starting)

Content Area Language Arts and Science

Instructional Value Vocabulary; life science

Text Structure Single letter

Title *Keeping Fit from A to Z: Mantente en Forma de la A a la Z*

Author Stephanie Maze

Photographer Various

Publishing Company/Date Moonstone Press/2014

ISBN# 978-0983498353

Summary This book is filled with over 150 vibrant, colorful photographs of kids in action, from sports to everyday activities. Photos surround each uppercase and lowercase letter, accompanied by a descriptive phrase in both English and Spanish. On some pages, the English comes first and dictates the letter of the alphabet associated with it; on other pages, the Spanish comes first; many, though, are cognates. All of the photos beautifully capture movement at its peak and will inspire readers to seek new and creative ways to stay active and be healthy. Another eight pages in the back of the book offers, in both English and Spanish, a list of other activities, games, and interesting facts in alphabetical order.

ELP Level 1 (beginning or starting)

Content Area Language Arts

Instructional Value Vocabulary

Text Structure Single letter

Title *Alphabet Fiesta*

Author Anne Miranda

Illustrator Schoolchildren

Publishing Company/Date Turtle Books/2001

ISBN# 978-1890515294

Summary In this bilingual story, many animals prepare for a surprise birthday party for Zelda the Zebra. Each letter is presented in both capital and lowercase in the upper left corner. A largely alliterative paragraph is shown in English first and then translated into Spanish below. The entry for A reads, "One sunny day in April, Armando the armadillo received a special letter in the mail from the mother of Zelda the zebra. It was an absolutely adorable invitation to a surprise party for Zelda." Children created the colorful illustrations.

ELP Level 3 (intermediate or developing)

Content Area Language Arts

Instructional Value Alliteration

Text Structure Single letter (expanded)

Title *¡Marimba!: Animales from A to Z*

Author Pat Mora

Illustrator Doug Cushman

Publishing Company/Date Clarion Books/2006

ISBN# 978-0618194537

Summary The ting-tong of the monkey's marimba awakens the zoo animals and provides the beat for a huge dance party. In this bilingual text, a Spanish featured word is within an English text. Almost all of the Spanish words are English language cognates for animals. Some animals are familiar, like *coyotes*, *elefantes*, and *koalas*; others, like *ocelots* and *vicuñas*, are less so. The watercolor illustrations are bright and cheerful, and the monkey who orchestrated the party appears in many of the illustrations. The two-line text on each page forms a gentle rhyme with the neighboring page. The painted capital letter is colorful and has some decorative element, like a series of dots along one side.

ELP Level 2 (high beginning or emerging)
Content Area Language Arts
Instructional Value Alphabetic principle
Text Structure Single letter (expanded)

Title *Just in Case: A Trickster Tale and Spanish Alphabet Book*
Author/Illustrator Yuyi Morales
Publishing Company/Date Roaring Book Press/2008
ISBN# 978-1596423298
Summary Searching through the alphabet for a present for Grandma Beetle, Señor Calavera, a not-too-scary skeleton from the Day of the Dead celebrations, learns that the greatest gift is love and companionship. Each letter is presented in capital form as the start of a Spanish word, followed by an English definition. Spanish words include *acordeón* (accordion), *bigote* (moustache), and *cosquillas* (tickles). Spanish words for CH and Ñ are also included. The dreamlike, jewel-toned illustrations include tiny white dots that appear to sparkle and lend an air of magic and movement, especially when Grandpa is reunited with Grandma at the end of the story.
ELP Level 2 (high beginning or emerging)
Content Area Language Arts
Instructional Value Vocabulary
Text Structure Single letter

Title *Un Paseo por el Bosque Lluvioso: A Walk in the Rainforest*
Author/Illustrator Kristin Joy Pratt
Publishing Company/Date Dawn Publications/1993
ISBN# 978-1878265531
Summary Written and illustrated when the author was just 15, this book brings a forward-thinking, young, ecology-minded perspective to the lush, exotic world of the rain forest. Each capital letter is set in a frame within the colorful illustration. An alliterative phrase, in both English and Spanish, introduces the word and is followed by an informative paragraph, also presented in both languages. The purpose of the book is to promote environmental awareness.
ELP Level 3 (intermediate or developing)
Content Area Language Arts and Science
Instructional Value Vocabulary; earth science; life science
Text Structure Conceptual text

Title *Pequeño Museo: Little Museum*
Author/Illustrator Alain Le Saux and Grégoire Solotareff
Publishing Company/Date Corimbo/2004

ISBN# 978-8484701705

Summary Each lowercase letter of the alphabet begins a single word on the left-hand page (Spanish first and English below), which is paired with a work of art on the right-hand page that illustrates the word. The artwork includes paintings from the 15th to 20th centuries. For the letter A, the following words are presented: *águila* (eagle), *anillo* (ring), *árbol* (tree), *ardilla* (squirrel), *arquerro* (archer), *asno* (donkey), and *autopistas* (freeways). A description of the artwork is in a smaller font at the bottom of the left-hand page. The selected artwork is a clear example of the topic word.

ELP Level 1 (beginning or starting)

Content Area Fine Art

Instructional Value Observation and perception

Text Structure Single letter

Title *ABeCedarios: Mexican Folk Art ABCs in English and Spanish*

Author Cynthia Weill

Photographer K. B. Basseches

Publishing Company/Date Cinco Puntos Press/2007

ISBN# 978-1933693132

Summary Showcasing the colorful, hand-painted wooden animal sculptures made by an Oaxacan family, each letter of the alphabet is presented on a brightly colored page with the wooden carving in the center. The animals are in active poses, crouching or sticking out their tongues. The name of the animal appears below in both English and Spanish, with the first letter of the animal's name in boldface and capitalized. All of the animals' names begin with the same English and Spanish letter, and a few extra animals are included for the Spanish digraphs CH and LL.

ELP Level 1 (beginning or starting)

Content Area Science

Instructional Value Cognates

Text Structure Single letter

Librarians' Link

Within the stacks of today's public school libraries, both print and digital resources abound for English Language Learners and their teachers.

- The *NTC's Dictionary of Spanish Cognates Thematically Organized,* by Nash (1999), contains over 20,000 Spanish–English cognates organized under everyday topics, such as "food" or "communications."

- *First Thousand Words in English,* by Heather Amery (2003), presents entertaining illustrations, along with the first thousand words that most children learn in English. *First Thousand Words* also exists in Spanish and in Chinese.

Notable Web Sites

Listed below are Web sites that contain instructional suggestions for English Language Learners.

http://www.esdict.com/English-Spanish-Cognates.htr

Listing true English–Spanish cognates by topics such as "nouns" and "fruits," this very helpful Web site possesses a user-friendly format in which brief paragraphs of suggestions for using cognates in writing are presented. All English Language Learners and instructors have a powerful tool with this Web site.

http://www.littleexplorers.com/languages/Spanishdictionary.html

With cute, colorful visuals to aid comprehension, this Web site houses an English–Spanish picture dictionary. For beginning English Language Learners, this enjoyable Web site builds an essential bridge in learning English.

http://spanishcognates.org

Containing a lot of helpful and valuable information for English Language learners, this Web site boasts inclusive lists of true cognates, arranged alphabetically. Supplying informative differentiations between true and false English–Spanish cognates, this easy-to-navigate and well-organized Web site is a must for all English Language Learners and their teachers.

http://www.teachersfirst.com/content/esl/

This friendly Web site provides lesson plans, Web resources, and curriculum units. There is a link for suggestions and classroom ideas for teaching English as a Second Language. Teachers will appreciate the wonderful array of classroom ideas and suggestions to enhance their teaching.

http://www.tesol.org

This Web site houses information about the professional educational association Teachers of English to Speakers of Other Languages. Presenting multiple formats of assistance to teachers of ELLs, this useful, organized Web site includes lesson plans, journal articles, blogs, conferences, and legal and political forums. This Web site should be bookmarked by every educator.

Works Cited

Blanchfield, C., and G. Tompkins. *Teaching Vocabulary: 50 Creative Strategies, Grades 6–12*. 2nd edition. Boston, MA: Pearson, 2007. Print.

Echevarria, J., M. Vost, and D. J. Short. *Making Content Comprehensible for English Language Learners: The SIOP Model*. Boston, MA: Pearson, 2008. Print.

Jennifer Sommer Homepage. 2016. Web. January 4. http://jennifersommer.weebly.com/

Migration Policy Institute Homepage. 2016. Web. February 25. http://www.migrationpolicy .org/

Palmer, B. C., V. S. Shackelford, S. C. Miller, and J. T. Leclere. "Bridging Two Worlds: Reading Comprehension, Figurative Language Instruction, and the English Language Learner." *Journal of Adolescent and Adult Literacy* 50 (4) (2007): 258–267. Print.

Pitcher, S., and B. Mackey. *Collaborating for Real Literacy: Librarian, Teacher, Literacy Coach and Principal.* 2nd edition. Santa Barbara, CA: Linworth, 2013. Print.

Reutzel, D. R., and R. B. Cooter. *The Essentials of Teaching Children to Read: The Teacher Makes the Difference.* Boston: Pearson, 2013. Print.

Spanish Cognates Homepage. 2016. Web. February 6. http://spanishcognates.org/

Teachers First Homepage. 2016. Web. January 5. http://teachersfirst.com/

Teachers of English to Speakers of Other Languages Homepage. 2016. Web. January 22. http://www.tesol.org/

Chapter 7

Zigzagging to the End

As a child, my number one best friend was the librarian in my grade school.
I actually believed she owned all those books in the library.
Erma Bombeck

The road for the creation of the English alphabet was not linear. The journey zigzagged through centuries and across continents. The wonder of written letters becoming composed, altered, sometimes adapted, and finally agreed upon by a specific culture engenders true excitement, as humans can speak, laugh, whisper, and shout endless varieties of words formed by those written letters. For the moment, the English alphabet has come to rest, with millions of people daily using her 26 letters in infinite communication formats.

The road for the creation of alphabet books was not linear. The journey zigzagged through centuries and across continents. From humble beginnings of black-and-white text or outdoor children's rhyming songs, alphabet books adapted and expanded, as did childhood and civilizations. The roadmap included hornbooks, battledores, and primers, with Dick and Jane waving them forward. Alphabet books represent a part of everyone's childhood, a shared experience that connects across geographic borders and language intersections.

The road for learning the alphabet is not linear. The journey zigzags through phonemic awareness, the alphabetic principle, nursery rhymes, and alphabet books. Along the way, dads read aloud about apple pie and acrobats, silly sneakers, and zany zebras before a goodnight hug. Around the bend, moms write grocery lists that hang on the fridge, capturing those crazy, squiggly marks that children see and try to copy. Soon, the thrill of being able to print those powerful letters shines in each child's mind and memory, empowering and enlightening. Please see figure 7.1.

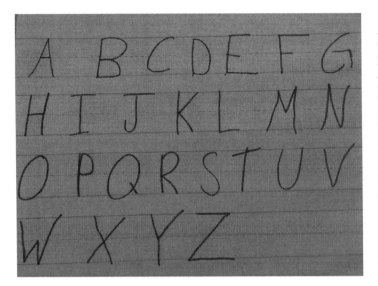

Figure 7.1   A Child's Handwritten Alphabet

The road for learning is not linear. The journey zigzags from family to school, crossing the dirt paths to park swings, browsing the library shelves, and finding fact signs while talking to ducks and gorillas at the zoo. Following the map to Grandma's house, traversing the countryside, and visiting international communities, the journey for learning zigzags forward, around, and sideways but always gathers knowledge, as butterflies gather nectar from the field flowers. The journey excites, exalts, and exhilarates. The journey has just begun, and the wonderful alphabet swings the doors wide open for us all.

Index

About the Authors

DR. BONNIE MACKEY received her PhD from Texas A&M University in 1998 and retired as an associate professor from the University of Houston–Clear Lake in 2015. During her career, she has taught several thousand college students and several hundred elementary students. Her love of children's books was sparked by her wonderment as young children experienced the joy of reading under her tutelage. Having raised three children and currently being a Nana to her granddaughters, she recognizes the importance of child self-selected books and the varying approaches that children need and use when learning to read.

With Dr. Sharon Pitcher, she has coauthored two books on literacy in the schools. Their first book was entitled *Collaborating for Real Literacy: Librarian, Teacher, and Principal* (Linworth Publishing Company, 2004). They published a second edition, *Collaborating for Real Literacy: Librarian, Teacher, Literacy Coach, and Principal* (ABC-CLIO, 2013). In addition, Dr. Mackey coauthored with her daughter, Jennifer Mackey Stewart, a book that combines her interests of gardening and literacy. This book, entitled *A Librarian's Guide to Cultivating an Elementary School Garden,* was published by Linworth in 2009.

HEDY SCHILLER WATSON received her BA in art history from the University of Virginia and an MBA from George Mason University. Having worked in museums and galleries, she has especially enjoyed the visual analysis of the alphabet books that she and Dr. Mackey reviewed. Her experience with teaching in an ESL (English as a Second Language) classroom and individual tutoring has broadened her knowledge of and approach to language learning at any age. She and her husband, Jim, are the proud parents of two teenagers.